LONDON CITY AIRPORT

30 years serving the capital

LONDON CITY AIRPORT

30 years serving the capital

Malcolm Ginsberg

A Very Big Thank You

My most sincere gratitude to Sharon Ross for her major contribution to the editorial and Alan Lathan, once of Jeppesen Airway Manuals, for his knowledge of the industry and diligence in proofing this tome. This list is far from complete but these are some of the people whose reminiscences and memories have helped me compile a book that is, I hope, a true reflection of a remarkable achievement. London City Airport – LCY to its friends and the travelling public – is a great success, and for London too. My grateful thanks go to all the contributors to this book, and in particular the following: Andrew Scott and Liam McKay of London City Airport; and the retiring Chief Executive Declan Collier, without whose support the project would never have got off the ground.

Tom Appleton	Ex-de Havilland Canada
Sir Philip Beck	Ex-John Mowlem & Co Plc (Chairman)
Pat Byrne	CityJet Executive Chairman
Alison Chambers	Emerald Media
Dermot Desmond	Previous owner of London City Airport
David Dorman	Dorway Public Relations on behalf of BAe Systems
Guy Douglas	Embraer
John Garwood	Canary Wharf Plc
Pandora George	Bullet PR for Royal Docks Management Authority
Roy Griffins	Ex-London City Airport (Chairman)
Ian Harbison	Air Transport Publications
Stuart Innes	Ex-London Docklands Development Corporation
Mike Johnson	Ex-Brymon Airways
Alan Lathan	Ex-Jeppesen
Mike Luddy	The Royal Docks Ltd
David Peglar	ExCeL London
James Rees	ExCeL London
Bob Schumacher	Ex-Eurocity Express (now with United Airlines)

And finally, I would like to thank my wife Linda who has followed my interest in London City Airport from the very beginning and for her patience with me while I was creating this book.

Photographs
Many thanks to Dave Williams of Express Photo Services who has recorded LCY from the beginning, for over 20 years, and has been very generous with his time in helping us locate photographs for this book. Also Vic Abbott, a NATS control tower engineer, also with the airport virtually from the beginning, and a keen snapper too; plus veteran photographers Mike Hooks, Peter March and Barry Wheeler.

We are indebted to *The Times* for the use of its extensive photo library for the Timeline chapter and London City Airport for its archives. Our thanks also to the Docklands Museum, the Royal Docks Group and Royal Wharf for the map on pages 184/5; and the Bruce McClaren Foundation in New Zealand who managed to find an image of Chris Amon and his pal Bill Bryce.

Malcolm Ginsberg

Published by Business Travel News Ltd 2017

PO Box 758, Edgware HA8 4QF, United Kingdom

www.btnews.co.uk

ISBN 978-1-900438-07-0

Produced by Forty Editorial Services Ltd

Printed at Short Run Press, Exeter, United Kingdom

Distributed by Crécy Publishing Ltd
www.crecy.co.uk

CONTENTS

E190-E2
E2
EMBRAER

FOREWORD

Sir Terry Morgan CBE

Chairman of London City Airport

I was delighted to be asked, and to accept the position as Chairman of London City Airport in March 2017. The airport, in my view, is the heartbeat of business flying in London.

The fact that we are celebrating the 30th anniversary of London City Airport is down to the dedication of its staff, past and present, who make the airport tick and help us deliver what I consider to be an industry leading customer experience for our passengers.

My first personal interaction with London City Airport was just six years ago when I took a flight to Glasgow. LCY was a busy terminal but I was struck by the no fuss approach to transferring me through check-in, security and boarding the aircraft. No fuss to me as a passenger, but obviously based on attention to detail by the airport. I have travelled through LCY a number of times since then, always on business and every time the airport is busy. I look forward to my much closer relationship with the airport as we continue our growth plans based on a significant investment in new assets but maintaining attention to the needs of those using the airport.

As you'll read in this book, it has not always been easy for LCY – an airport in the Docklands was a bold and pioneering concept, and it has had to fight for its existence and its market share. I would like to use this foreword to say a personal thank you to Mowlem Construction, under the steerage of Sir Philip Beck, and previous Chairmen, including Roy Griffins, who readied the ground for growth and the dynamic business you see and use today.

Those challenges have been balanced in equal measure with opportunities, so much so that since the previous milestone of the 20th anniversary in 2007, the number of passengers using the airport has almost doubled, most recently to just over 4.5 million in 2016.

Looking to the future, what I see now for LCY is potential; significant potential for the airport, and across the whole of East London, which is experiencing incredible regeneration. In the coming decade East London will be at the centre of London's growth, its new homes, its new jobs, its new residents. And thanks to our City Airport Development Programme, LCY will play a key role in supporting that growth, attracting investment and connecting London businesses globally. As it once served Canary Wharf, I see the LCY of the future continuing to connect our traditional business hubs, but also emerging ones in Stratford, Barking, Greenwich, Bexley and beyond.

And as we grow, we'll do so responsibly, continuously innovating so we balance the impact of our operations with the benefits of employment and economic growth. We will continue to invest in our communities so the people and school children of East London can take advantage of the opportunities we create.

It's an exciting time to be part of London City Airport. On behalf of myself, the shareholders and management team I'd like to thank you for your support and custom. We now look to the future and to building an airport that not only meets your expectations, but exceeds them.

July 2017

Now and Then

30 Years of Travel and London City Airport

2017	1987
Canadian-led consortium owners	John Mowlem & Co
Newham Council	London Docklands Development Corporation
Runway length 1199m	Runway length 762m
Airbus A318 (largest aircraft)	Dornier 228 (smallest)
Embraer E Series (main aircraft)	BAe 146 (ready to come in)
Bombardier CS	Dash 7
BBC *EastEnders* map shows London City	BBC *EastEnders* map (London City was refused)
Theresa May	Margaret Thatcher
Chris Grayling	Paul Channon (both Secretary of State for Transport)
Rob Sinclair – Airport CEO	John Douthwaite – Airport Director
11 airline operators	Two scheduled airlines
50 destinations from London City Airport	Three destinations from London City Airport
Maximum 45 runway movements per hour	15 runway movements per hour
Policemen with guns	George Dixon style bobbie
App	Ticket coupon
Docklands Light Railway	North London Line
Oyster card	Bus ticket
Body security scanner	Ticket inspection
London City to Paris Orly	London City to Paris Charles de Gaulle
Greater London Authority from 2000	Greater London Council (GLC) disbanded 1986
Sadiq Khan – Mayor of London	No London leader with the axing of the GLC
One pound coin	One pound note
European red biometric passport	British printed blue passport
Wi-fi	Fax
Shop till you drop at London City Airport	Single coffee shop at London City Airport
Smartphone	Telephone kiosk
Electronic flight bag for pilots	Flight manual
Drone	Helicopter photo ship
GPS	Find your position on a map or use a compass
iPad	Notepad
Low voltage chargers	Three (and two) pin plugs
Kindle	Books (but we still do have them)
Smart screens	Noticeboards
34.3 million cars in Britain	20.5 million cars in Britain
United Kingdom population 66 million	United Kingdom population 57 million

INTRODUCTION

March 1982. London was its usual self. Wet, dull and miserable. I was in my then City office. I had resigned from Lotus Cars and my first clients as a public relations practitioner were Colin Chapman's Moonraker boat company, CSE-The Oxford Air Training School and Plymouth-based Brymon Airways.

The phone rang. It was Bill Bryce, the enigmatic owner and Managing Director of Brymon. At that time BC (our two-letter airline code) was an up and coming British regional carrier and had just taken delivery of the first UK-registered 50-seat de Havilland Canada Dash 7 short take-off and landing aircraft. Bill and I had both flown on the aircraft at the Farnborough Air Show in 1978 and were impressed. Subsequently Brymon operated a Plymouth to Heathrow service, as well as basing a pair of aircraft at Aberdeen in support of the offshore oil activities.

'Be a good fellow and pop down to Heron Quays and see if we can land an aircraft there,' Bill said in his New Zealand drawl. Heron Quays I thought to myself. That's south of Whitechapel. Docklands. Or dying Docklands by then. 'Some crazy guy has called me to say the Dash 7 might be able to get down on a disused dock,' he said. It seemed that Philip Beck, a private pilot, had noticed in *Flight International* magazine a report of the aircraft's astonishing short field performance.

What I saw was around 1,000 yards of abandoned quay, free of obstacles at each end. As a former private pilot myself it seemed to me that the Dash 7 might safely make a landing but it was up to the professionals to take a proper look and for the Civil Aviation Authority to approve a flight. I also drove to the proposed site of an airport in the derelict King George V Dock and visualised what might happen. But it did seem a long way from the City of London.

This book will take you through the history of what is now London City Airport and still the only active purpose-built UK airport built since World War II. No one person or event can take the plaudits for its undoubted success. Politicians nearly wrecked it but those with vision and enterprise stood by the project in its darkest days. The Docklands Light Railway (DLR) has arrived and hopefully the Elizabeth Line (Crossrail) for the future. Some 4.5 million passengers used the airport in 2016 and it is part of the new city that is Canary Wharf and the Isle of Dogs. ExCeL, London's leading exhibition centre, sits adjoining the site, 60 destinations are served and New York, Moscow and the Gulf states are now within the scope of non-stop scheduled flights.

Do take a look at Heron Quays next time you are at Canary Wharf. There is a plaque at ground level as you enter the DLR station to commemorate the test landing on 29 June 1982. Things have changed somewhat since then!

Created by Margaret Thatcher's incoming Conservative Government, the London Docklands Development Corporation (LDDC) had been tasked with rejuvenating a part of East London that appeared to have no future. Under the energetic leadership of Reg Ward, the LDDC took over an 8.5-square mile area of East London, nominally called 'The Docklands', including parts of Newham, Tower Hamlets and Southwark. The task to turn it into a 21st century mini-city. London City Airport is a lasting tribute to Reg Ward and his innovative team.

Malcolm Ginsberg
London
July 2017

Prince Philip and London City Airport

From the time of its first landing in July 1988 the British Aerospace (BAe) 146, and its successor the Avro RJ, have provided the backbone of aircraft operations at LCY. CityJet expects to use the four-engined aircraft, with a capacity of up to 112 passengers, into the next decade.

A one-time pilot Prince Philip, a keen supporter of LCY and the 146, is seen here in the BAe Hatfield simulator before being put through his paces.

As part of preparations for the 2017 anniversary, a special pamphlet from the tenth anniversary of the airport in 1997 was rediscovered which demonstrated that the airport had royal approval.

In a foreword Prince Philip, wrote: 'The Queen opened London City Airport 10 years ago and I can only imagine that the developers must have held their breath as they waited to see whether this somewhat unconventional airport was going to be a success. I think it was a brilliant idea, but then I found it to be wonderfully convenient. I once made it in 19 minutes from Buckingham Palace.'

Recently Buckingham Palace was able to confirm to the author of this book 'That he [His Royal Highness] was in the cockpit for a number of flights into, and out of, London City Airport', his Private Secretary noting that 'This letter comes with Prince Philip's best wishes.'

Above: *Often seen for training purpose in the early days, on short finals at LCY, a No 32 (Royal) Squadron BAe 146.*

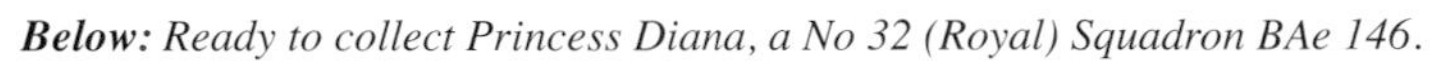

Below: *Ready to collect Princess Diana, a No 32 (Royal) Squadron BAe 146.*

THE AIRPORT DIRECTORS

(Chief Executive Officers)

John Douthwaite (*left*). 1986–1988. With some of the first passengers.

Bill Lindsell (*left*). 1988–1990. Seen here with the Duke of Kent.

Bill Charnock. 1990–1995

John Horne. 1995–1996

Richard Gooding, OBE. 1996–2012

Declan Collier. 2012–2017

Chapter One
Reflections on London City Airport

Declan Collier

The selection of Declan Collier as Chief Executive of London City Airport in March 2012, following the retirement of Richard Gooding after 15 years, was seen by both the City and the air travel industry as a determination by the airport owner to make an appointment of real standing in the international airport forum. Previously Chief Executive of the State-owned Dublin Airport Authority since 2005, and prior to that with ExxonMobil, Declan is Chair of the World Board of Airport Council International (ACI), the airport equivalent body of IATA, and formerly Chair of ACI Europe. He holds a Masters degree from Trinity College Dublin.

Declan announced his decision to stand down in April 2017, his post taken by Robert Sinclair from Bristol Airport who joins London City exactly 30 years after Queen Elizabeth officially opened the terminal. Here he reflects on his five years in charge whilst Robert Sinclair considers the challenges ahead as the airport moves towards a new era.

'In one of my first interviews as CEO of London City Airport a journalist from the *Daily Telegraph* speculated that LCY would feel like an oasis of calm after the DAA. Well, I can happily say it has been anything but, instead it has been a time characterised by growth, by change and by significant achievement.

In early 2012 we were a business of around 1,400 staff, eight airlines and around three million passengers. We were a business that was rightly proud of the fast, efficient service it provided, in particular for the dynamic businesses of the City and Canary Wharf. But we wanted to do more and we had that potential.

The City Airport Development Programme (CADP) was a vision for our future airport; an airport that could meet demand, welcome the next generation of aircraft, connect to new global destinations and not only serve London's financial, business and government districts, but be a catalyst for the regeneration of East London.

This was an ambitious programme, and one that we undertook at the most challenging period in UK aviation. Despite having a compelling case, there were setbacks, significant ones, which at times led me to question whether CADP was deliverable.

But, what inspired me was how steadfast and committed our whole business was to overcoming the obstacles that had been placed in front of us. We knew we had a winning case, and despite the headwinds of exiting the European Union and a change in political leadership, in July 2016, CADP was consented by the UK Government.

We were vindicated, but more importantly, it allowed us to plan for the future; a future in which we would create another 2,000 new jobs, add much needed capacity to the UK aviation system and generate £1.3 billion for the UK economy each year.

Change is part and parcel of any business and LCY has had two owners in my time at the airport. While sales processes are never easy, what has struck me was the belief our respective owners have in the airport, their willingness to invest and their certainty in our potential.

"Faster, Better Journeys" is our vision. It is a proposition that I believe sets us apart from all other UK and EU airports and we invest heavily to provide the best passenger experience.

I would take up the rest of the book if I were to list all that we have done in this time, but instead let me characterise how we embraced change and innovation and built an airport with our customers at its heart.

If you walked down our West Pier two years ago you would be reminded of the days of 50-seater aircraft serving the airport, so we invested £24 million in an upgrade programme to handle 100-seat+ aircraft, adding more seats, more space and new concessions for our customers.

Alongside this we have constantly looked at ways of not only maintaining our '20/15' passenger proposition. It takes just 20 minutes from disembarking the DLR to getting to your gate. And on arrivals it is 15 minutes from landing to arriving at the DLR. As we are a small, agile company we have been able to work with emerging London and UK tech companies like CrowdVision and Autonoma who have allowed us to measure train-to-gate real time passenger flows and embrace Artificial Intelligence solutions in the aircraft turnaround process. Passenger insight allows us to make dynamic, informed decisions that in an LCY context, means an ever quicker, better airport experience.

And, most recently, we were able to announce a UK first, a Digital Remote Control Tower. This again demonstrated that LCY was resolutely cutting edge and the Tower, once complete in 2019, will create a more reliable and resilient service that by embracing new technology, will make LCY even more efficient and directly benefit our passengers.

As I look at the business now, we are an airport that is building from a position of strength. And don't take just my word for it, look at the litany of awards and recognition the team has received, from the best airport in the world under five million passengers in 2017 by Skytrax, to gaining stage 3 Carbon Accreditation Status from ACI Europe, to winning the inaugural UK All Party Corporate Social Responsible Business of the year award.

What these successes say to me is that we are an airport that is ready for the future. We are an airport about to embark on a £370 million development programme, an airport that is poised to double its workforce to 4,500 by the mid-2020s and an airport that is ready to welcome more airlines and the newest, most innovative aircraft.

We are also an airport that, just as when we opened on 5 November 1987, is steadfastly committed to investing in, and creating opportunities for, our local community. This is an East London business and it will continue to create jobs for its residents, invest in their education and continue to be an industry leader in noise and environmental mitigation.

There is much to look forward to. London City Airport, the only London airport actually in London, is set to serve the capital for a further 30 years, and beyond.'

And a few words from Robert Sinclair

Robert Sinclair comes to London City Airport as Chief Executive Officer after a similar position at Bristol Airport since 2008. During his time Bristol Airport has seen record growth in passenger numbers and profitability and the successful delivery of a £160 million development programme.

A native of New Zealand, Mr Sinclair is a qualified chartered accountant and solicitor. Prior to taking on the role at Bristol he was the Chief Financial Officer of Auckland International Airport following a ten-year career with UBS in investment banking.

'I am delighted to be taking on the role of Chief Executive Officer of LCY on the occasion of its 30th anniversary and at such an exciting time for the airport.

I would like to pay tribute to Declan and the whole team for all their hard work in getting LCY to where it is today – an award-winning, incredibly popular airport right in the heart of London. We have a very ambitious development programme ahead of us – a plan to increase capacity to 6.5 million passengers per year and 111,000 flight movements, much needed capacity when the rest of the London airport market is highly constrained and congested, and at a time when the City of London and the UK must protect and grow international connectivity.

While expanding the airport's capacity, we will continue to deliver an outstanding customer experience both on departure and arrival, and infuse our airport with a real sense of place, recognising our very distinctive East London heritage and location. It's going to be a huge challenge, but one that I am very excited about.'

Tom Appleton

It was back in 1966 Tom Appleton joined the then de Havilland Canada (DHC), now Bombardier, becoming a senior development pilot famously demonstrating the Dash 7's remarkable runway performance at Farnborough 1978. He served as Vice-President of Customer Support of Bombardier Amphibious and later VP for the sale of its products around the world. As CEO of Piaggio Aero Industries SpA he was much involved with the development of the Avanti turboprop. He is a Director of Conair Group Inc, the British Columbia company specialising in airborne firefighting. Tom Appleton is Chairman of the Canadian Aviation Hall of Fame.

In many ways without Tom Appleton's guidance Brymon Airways would not have survived serious financial problems. He reflects on the past and looks at the future.

'Bill Bryce was a regular visitor to the de Havilland plant at Toronto (Canada) during the late seventies purchasing one after the other of our Twin Otter utility aircraft to be used mainly on routes out of Plymouth. Like all our guests he was impressed with the Dash 7 when he flew on it at Farnborough and when the opportunity to purchase the aircraft came about shortly afterwards he quickly put a package together.

Perhaps too quick. In truth Brymon was in no shape to take on the investment required of such a daring venture, both a new very advanced aircraft, and what was effectively a new airport.

Having purchased Dash 7s with financing in Dollars, the airline was soon faced with a recession and the collapse of the Pound. Repayment of its debt was impossible and in 1983 de Havilland Canada, as the largest creditor, called in the auditors Peat Marwick to devise a strategy.

DHC's anxieties about the likely collapse of Brymon were twofold. First was a commitment to our good customers Chevron and Shell, worldwide operators of DHC aircraft supporting their exploration programmes, who relied on Brymon Dash 7s to transport their North Sea employees from Aberdeen to the Unst Heliport, in the Shetland Isles.

DHC's second concern was the embryonic, but much longer term opportunity presented at London Docklands.

As one of the test pilots involved in the original development of the Dash 7, including participation with the British contribution to the certification standards created for short take-off and landing (STOL) operations of the Dash 7, with its 7.5-degree approach slope approval, I had maintained close contact with Brymon as it expanded its regional services.

When the company's problems surfaced, DHC President John Sandford dispatched me overnight to London with instructions to "sort it out". With our advisors, we worked out a plan to hold off on bankruptcy proceedings and keep Brymon afloat on its cash flow to await better business conditions, if the regulator could be convinced to approve it. The Civil Aviation Authority was receptive to our proposal and allowed DHC temporary dispensation to own and operate the UK-based airline for a limited period, to save 400 jobs in Plymouth and perhaps see the Docklands development forward.

We immediately purchased the Brymon assets from Bill Bryce (for just £100,000, if I remember correctly) the night before bankruptcy would have been unavoidable.

The first task was to find a professional manager to run the airline, so DHC Chairman "Barney" Danson, the former Canadian Defence Minister, arranged a meeting with Margaret Thatcher's "favourite businessman", ICI and British Airways' Chairman Sir John (later Lord) King, in his offices in the City.

When asked if he could recommend a CEO to head up Brymon, Sir John responded from behind his massive desk in a cloud of smoke from his Churchillian cigar: "You could do worse than to read this morning's *Financial Times*."

BA had just fired in spectacular fashion, noted as "the night of the long knives", several redundant executives from the BOAC/ BEA merger that produced British Airways! Amongst those names, although he had resigned BA earlier in frustration, was Charles Stuart, a former BEA executive who had headed up the regional operations, including Northeast Airways based in Newcastle. We quickly formed a new board with myself as Managing Shareholder, a way of satisfying the British Government regarding overseas ownership at the time. Over the next three years Charles and I, with the same vision for Brymon, never had a disagreement that wasn't resolved privately and quickly! The Canadian ownership was something that was never aired in public.

As Mowlem and the London Docklands Development Corporation pressed on with the development in the docks Brymon built up a network of services across the UK and on my visits to Plymouth I could transfer with some satisfaction into Terminal One and the service to Devon and Cornwall.

At the very end of 1985 we entered negotiations with Sir Colin (later Lord) Marshall, Chief Executive of British Airways, that resulted in DHC's divestiture of the company to BA and the Brymon management. The Brymon investment cost British Airways just £500,000 for a company that included up to five pairs of the Heathrow slots!

The Docklands airport was by now well on its way and interest from other airlines inevitably followed when Sir Michael (also later raised to the Lords) Bishop in 1987 established London City Airways with new Dash 7s bought directly from DHC.

It can be argued that without the Dash 7 there would be no London City Airport.

Today the Dash 7's successor, the twin-engined Bombardier Q400 is a mainstay of the airport and for the future the Bombardier C Series will open up new non-stop routes thought impossible 30 years ago. I hope in the future to be able to plan a trip from New York to London City Airport, with an inspection, and then on to Moscow or perhaps Doha.'

Tom Appleton
Toronto
July 2017

Sir Philip Beck

'When I became Chairman of John Mowlem and Company in 1979, I was very aware that a major area of work for Mowlem – based on our maintenance contract for the Port of London Authority (PLA) – was in steep decline largely because of containerisation in the shipping industry.

It was in that context that I met the newly appointed Chief Executive of the London Docklands Development Corporation, Reg Ward, for lunch at a restaurant called L'Opera near Covent Garden.

At the end of this lunch, talking mainly about the inner docks, St Katherine and Canary Wharf, I asked Reg what his thoughts were for the most easterly of the Docks, The Royal Docks.

Reg replied that he saw the Royal Docks as a Transport Interchange and Hub, because they were well equipped with existing rail tracks and were close to the North and South Circular Roads, together with the then proposed construction of another Thames road crossing at Beckton.

My immediate thought, which I expressed to Reg was that in 1980 a full-function transport interchange had to include an airport. He, straight away, got the point and said he knew exactly where it could and should go. On the long peninsula between the King George V Dock and the Royal Albert Dock. And that is where London City Airport is today.

From that small beginning it took almost a decade to get to the opening of LCY in 1987, through planning, negotiation with the PLA, the public planning enquiry, and then its construction. We were very pleased to welcome HM The Queen to open the airport.

At first growth was slow, but gradually passenger numbers increased. The confidence in our LCY investment by my then colleagues on Mowlem's board mostly relied on the experts we had employed to tell us how many passengers we could expect to use LCY.

I had always thought that an airport close to the City would be a part of the natural monopoly comprising the London airport system, and so in the medium term would inevitably prosper.

We had long sought a partner in this airport project, and the then nationalised owner of all the other London airports was keen to invest, but the Department of Transport forbade it to do so. So, after I retired from Mowlem's chairmanship in 1996, the new Chairman and Board decided to sell the airport and was only able to realise a truly pathetic price from the more far sighted Dermot Desmond. To be fair, Mowlem's share price reacted favourably to the news of the sale.

However a decade further on, the whole of Mowlem was sold for £350 million and LCY alone in the same year for over £700 million.

I am proud to have been one of the main instigators of London City Airport, but of course there were others, even just within Mowlem, who played a greater part in its becoming the success it is today, such as Roger Sainsbury, Bill Lindsell and Bill Charnock.

Who would have thought in 1988, when we carried just 133,000 passengers, that this year that figure would reach towards five million.'

Sir Philip Beck
London
July 2017

Pat Byrne

'My abiding memories of London City Airport have their origin in 1988 when I chartered a Dornier 228 to do "a proving flight" into, what had been drawn to my attention by the Chairman of the plc to whom I had recently sold my financial business, as 'that little airstrip down the docks'.

On reflection, we concluded it might be best to file the proving flight away and that maybe it would best be revisited when the runway was lengthened to take jets. Fast forward to Autumn 1992, and the airport came back on the horizon but this time in the context of a plan for an airline with LCY as the pivotal focus of the business. Work was well underway on building a tunnel which would facilitate improved road access from the City. But my main interest at the time was looking across the river from the Terminal building at the DLR Silvertown station and wondering what would it take to bring that link to the airport and by when?

Move the dial again to 10 January 1994 and, in the company of Richard Branson, I am having my photo taken as we launched the inaugural CityJet scheduled service to Dublin from LCY. Mr Branson was present because we agreed to rent his brand on the tail to secure us early traction as a start-up from a relatively equally unknown little airport with a "downtown" postal address.

As Murphy's Law tends to work, that launch day coincided with the Rotherhide Tunnel being closed due to urgent repairs being required and the Mother of all traffic jams ensued. Unknown to any of us, a number of Irish newspapers had set up their own private "air race" with journalists timing their access to the West End, utilising all five London airports, including of course LCY. The headlines the next day were not kind to us as we came in 'Paddy Last' in the 'Great Air Race'.

But being Irish we are familiar with reruns (Theresa May please take note!) so we convinced the Irish national radio station, RTE, to organise another Great Air Race a week later. On this occasion we won it by the proverbial 'country mile' – breaking the winning tape by a full hour over the next placed airport.

The rest, as they say is history; but what a history – one of delivering millions of passengers through this unique gateway into London. That is the real story.

Over the subsequent 24 years, CityJet has continued to operate services out of LCY to European cities and the airline has played a major part in placing this airport firmly to the forefront as the London airport of choice for not just the business traveller but also the discerning leisure passengers who place sufficient value on their time and their physical wellbeing to avoid the scrum of other London airports and the endless trek from plane to City.

Of course, over such a long period of activity at LCY we have experienced many challenges when the weather has not always facilitated travel and the restricted opening hours (in compliance with the very demanding local environmental sensitivities) have conspired to deny us access to our "aircraft carrier" in the Thames Estuary on a limited number of occasions. However, our regular passengers have remained steadfast through the good times and the sometimes challenging times because they know that LCY still represents the easiest point of access to London by far.'

Pat Byrne
Dublin
July 2017

Dermot Desmond

'In June 1995, I was approached by CityJet Chief Executive Pat Byrne. He was seeking to open a new Dublin – Brussels route. I had no interest in investing in an embryonic airline due to their high rate of failures, but I told Pat that if it were possible I would happily invest in an airport.

I was a believer in airports as an investment class from my years as Chairman of the Irish Airports Authority (Aer Rianta). Equally I believed in the future of London Docklands and the ever-growing demand for air transport.

Pat told me that he felt Mowlem Plc was considering a sale of London City Airport and offered to set up a meeting with Mowlem's CEO John Marshall. I met with Mr Marshall a week later and we agreed, subject to the usual conditions, a deal to buy the airport for £30 million.

Following a period of due diligence, led by Arthur Andersen who advised against purchasing the airport, a revised deal was agreed with Mowlem in September 1995. At the time, there were only three airlines operating from London City and the future for two of these looked bleak. Happily, CityJet continues to fly through the airport to this day.

Equally, the only passenger jet certified to land at London City was the BAe 146. But again there was uncertainty over its future. Fokker had a jet going through trials, the Fokker 70, but with hindsight, Fokker had not much of a future either. Against this background, the deal closed on 28 October 1995.

Bill Charnock, who had passed retirement age, agreed to extend his stay for a year to enable me to recruit a new Chief Executive. I identified Richard Gooding, who was running Luton Airport, and between Richard and David Thompson, the Finance Director, I had the nucleus of a management team. Ray MacSharry agreed to come on board as the Chairman and my colleague Michael Walsh from International Investment and Underwriting also joined the Board of Directors.

Shortly after buying the airport I met with the Reichman Brothers, British Aerospace and the London Docklands Development Corporation (LDDC) – all pivotal players in the future of the airport and Canary Wharf and all were very supportive. We were extraordinarily fortunate in our timing. The airport generated cash from the day the purchase was completed and, despite the bombings in Canary Wharf, London City and the surrounding area have developed in parallel.

In 2002 we opened the Jet Centre to cater for the increase in private aviation and I was pleased to be one of their most frequent customers!

In 2006, I received an unsolicited approach to buy London City Airport at a valuation which appeared attractive. I decided that we should explore its true value in conjunction with Gavin McDonald and Colm Donlon of Morgan Stanley. They achieved a price 25% above the unsolicited offer and I was happy to accept. To put the worth in perspective, they realised a value for London City Airport which equated to a 50% interest in Gatwick, an airport with circa ten times more passengers.

Where do we go from here?

At all stages, my experience with London City has been positive and I am delighted that the new owners have developed the airport to where it is today, under the leadership of another Irishman, and has also managed to achieve a financial success for the investors.

I was delighted to see that within days of his appointment, the Chancellor of the Exchequer Philip Hammond was able to visit London City Airport and give the go-ahead for its expansion.

When we took over the airport 15 movements an hour were considered the maximum for the runway. For the future 45 movements per hour will be the maximum with no holding on the stand while another aircraft lands. The parallel taxiway will be a real boon for the airport not just for scheduled operations but executive jets as well.'

Dermot Desmond
Dublin
July 2017

Roy Griffins

Chairman of London City Airport Ltd for ten years to 2017, Roy Griffins completed a long governmental career mainly in the Department for Transport as Director-General of Civil Aviation 1999–2004. He was made a Companion of the Order of the Bath in the 2003 New Year's Honours list.

'Back in 2009 when a national newspaper described London City Airport as 'bijou and startlingly well run', I felt a certain pride because less than three years before I had been brought in by the airport's then brand new owners to chair the Board.

Actually, my personal connection with London City had started 20 years earlier, when, in 1987, I was private secretary and bag-carrier to the then Secretary of State for Transport as he (and I) accompanied HM The Queen when she opened London City Airport and then we all returned to Westminster Pier in the royal motor launch. I remember Her Majesty, characteristically well-briefed, in animated aviation-oriented conversation with my Ministerial charge as we chugged back up the Thames. London City has come a long way since then.

I also remember the arguments in the late eighties amongst senior transport officials about letting the presence of this interloper from the aviation sector interfere with grand plans for a series of road bridges across the docks and the river. An ambitious Highways Deputy-Secretary and his staff really resented being thwarted by the 'Biggles' team. Then there followed quite a struggle to move on from the Dash 7 to allow other aircraft types, and then jets(!) to use London City. But it happened, because the original concept of putting an airport where London City is was sound.

In September 2001, when New York's twin towers were destroyed in the 9/11 attacks and flights suspended across the north Atlantic, I was the Director of Aviation who signed the Order closing UK airspace. I well remember having to 'explain' with some force to London City's Chief Executive of the time why the ban had to stay a bit longer than he believed was reasonable.

By then, Mowlem had gone, and Dermot Desmond owned the airport. When, five years later, at the end of 2006, he sold London City to Global Infrastructure Partners and AIG for a sum which most observers of the aviation sector thought ludicrously high, that was the point where London City Airport really started growing up. Coming in as Chairman, the one thing that I was clear about was that London City needed to conduct itself just like the much bigger European airports, across the board – safety (of course), security, pricing, schedules, slot allocation, airspace use, and more. And we did just that.

So when HM The Queen, this time with Prince Philip, came back to London City a quarter of a century after her first visit, to celebrate the airport's 25th birthday, I was more than proud (of the place, not of myself) to accompany Her Majesty again around a piece of aviation infrastructure which indeed had grown to be one of the country's vital transport assets.

I admit to being a public transport geek, so I always travel to and from London City by the DLR, tube, and/or Overground. I love to listen to travellers expressing (pleasant) surprise about their experiences of the airport.

I am tempted to bore them with my message that London City is not like other airports. It is simply better. It honestly does what it is supposed to do. It works with its neighbours, with its customers (airlines and passengers), with its regulators, with government (local and national). It is a boon to East London, the capital, the country. I encourage London City's current owners to keep it that way. I am glad to have had a small part in the airport's first 30 years.'

Roy Griffins
London
July 2017

Reg Ward

By Stuart Innes

A lifetime civil servant Stuart Innes was seconded from the Department of Environment (DoE) to help the then Chief Executive designate, Reg Ward, establish a quasi-government organisation which then did not have a name or an office or any staff! Thus the London Docklands Development Corporation (LDDC) was born.

He stayed with the Corporation throughout the whole of its operational life working at different times as the Chief Executive's assistant, reorganising the LDDC's administration, social facilities, community development, community services joint planning and then finally in winding it all up in an orderly manner. He left the DoE on 'early retirement' in May 1998 but continued his involvement with the airport as Secretary of the London City Airport Consultative Committee from a steering group in 1986 until his final withdrawal in 2015. Stuart Innes could justifiably claim he knew Reg Ward better than most.

Here he reflects on Reg Ward and how perhaps he would have viewed today's London City Airport, and the Docklands.

Reg Ward (1927–2011) was the son of a miner, went to Manchester University and spent the first part of his career with Inland Revenue as a tax inspector. A series of local government appointments followed, culminating in him becoming Chief Executive of the London Borough of Hammersmith and Fulham, and later of Hereford and Worcester County Council.

'It is a strange world. In fact it was I who interviewed Reg for the job of Chief Executive of what was to become the London Docklands Development Corporation (LDDC) back in 1980 recommending him to my boss Michael Heseltine for the job. Clearly it was a two-way endorsement as one of his first steps on setting up the embryo organisation was to ask me to join him. The relationship was to become very father and son over a tumultuous eight years. "Why move to the middle of nowhere when you can move to the middle of London?" was a slogan he conjured up.

His approach was to seize opportunities whenever and wherever they arose. "You could say that Docklands is a 'happening', a happy coincidence of opportunity and accident," Reg used to say. "There have been no master plans or detailed development frameworks."

If Reg were here today and in charge of a much politically changed area with the local councils back in control he might take the lift to the One Canary Wharf marketing suite and take a look at the huge layout model of East London and ask a few questions. "What is going on here, here and here?" He would come up with a few ideas.

Crossrail was conceived after Reg's demise as the LDDC leader but he certainly watched its development in his retirement and would have supported the proposed SW/NE expansion. Reg was never able to fly from London City Airport to New York, which he regretted. He was able to show his support for London City Airport when in 2005 he came up from Stroud to unveil a tablet at Heron Quays station entrance commemorating Captain Harry Gee's first landing all those years earlier. It was a coming together of the Docklands Light Railway, Canary Wharf and London City Airport, three of his finest achievements.

Reg cultivated a team which I was proud to be part of.'

Stuart Innes
Wakefield
July 2017

Chapter Two
History of the London Docklands

What we now call the London Docklands was once known as Plaistow Marshes. West Ham United was born by the river as Thames Ironworks Football Club. Dick Turpin ruled the roost in the early 1700s, but he was not as romantic as we are led to believe, a horse thief executed in 1739 aged 33.

Today the area that we now call Docklands is thriving once again but it has had more than its fair share of ups and downs. On 5 November 1987 Queen Elizabeth officially opened London City Airport, the catalyst for one of the most successful regeneration programmes of modern times. After centuries of changes in social, economic and political conditions London to the east was about to see as dramatic a change as at any time in its 2,000 year history.

The name Londonium, what we now call London, was established by the Romans in 50 AD. Around where London Bridge now stands was the first practical crossing point of the River Thames to England's then capital Colchester. The port was highly valued as an import centre bringing in such luxuries as oil and wine.

London lost its energy when the Saxons came to power (from 410 AD), who preferred more provincial major towns. With the Norman Conquest (from 1066) and the building of the White Tower, what we now call the Docklands began to establish itself. But the area really began to flourish in the 'golden age' of the Elizabethan period (1558–1603) with the advancement of seaborne exploration leading to trade with previously unchartered lands such as Russia, India, Far East and Africa.

However, the rise, fall and eventual rise again of the riverside areas to the east of the Tower of London was not straightforward and the Civil War (1642–51), Great Plague (1665–66), and Great Fire (1666) meant that the Docklands was in a state of ruin and trade fell once again.

By the end of the next century the Docklands had re-established itself as a major port and trade was doubling every 30 years. What was to become the British Empire was being established at ports all around the globe supported from London. The docks were bursting at the seams. The increasing trade in the area had also brought with it piracy and a large number of unaccounted ships entering the port without paying their import taxes. For this reason, and also to compete with Bristol and Liverpool, an enclosed docks system was gradually introduced. It is this dock area which we know as the London Docklands today.

The virtue of the purpose-built docks was that loading and unloading could take place at any time with the water level always the same. Its disadvantage was that the ships had to use locks to arrive and depart from the tidal River Thames and only at specified times. It was to prove to be both its virtue and undoing. The massive container ships and cruise liners of today have found other ports as their home bases, the

The London docks at Wapping in 1808.

rise of Tilbury, Harwich and later Felixstowe, the home for the cargo carriers. Today Dover, Britain's busiest port, and Southampton, are the main gateways for sea-going holiday passengers.

In all, 11 docks were built between 1802 and 1921 with the final three, the Royal Albert Dock, the Royal Victoria Dock and the King George V Dock known as the Royal Docks. London City Airport stands on the King George V Dock. The Royal Docks provided berths for large vessels that could not be accommodated further up river, and became London's principal sea outlet during the first half of the 20th century.

In 1851 the Great Exhibition was held at what is now Hyde Park, the first ever World's Fair. An astonishing six million people visited the Crystal Palace, the centrepiece (later moved to Sydenham, South London, it burnt down in 1936). Many came by the railways, most of them never previously having ventured out of their small town or village.

The trains also came to Docklands.

By the 1850s, London's port comprised a number of docks owned by individual private dock companies. Housing, industry and commercial premises quickly surrounded these river docks, leaving little room for any expansion to meet the need of technological changes with the introduction of steam-powered ships. Low financial returns led to a lack of investment in new facilities and, at a time of rapid advances in what we now call technology, the Port of London's facilities became increasingly out-dated and inefficient. In Wapping and Limehouse the docks were far from fit for purpose almost as soon as they were dug, unable to cope with the ever larger ships made possible by the age of steam.

In contrast, the Royal Docks were at the forefront of technology for a good many years and enjoyed a long period of prosperity. The Victoria Dock (receiving its Royal prefix in 1880) with its hydraulically-powered equipment and direct access to the railway system being an immediate success.

By 1886 there were seven enclosed dock systems within the Port of London, the West India, St Katherine (1805–28) with narrow entrance channels and very limited capacity compared with the Royals, East India (1805), Surrey (1807), Millwall (1868), and finally the Royal Docks (1855–1921) themselves. Down river Tilbury opened in 1886.

Stevedores at work.

Although the Port of London grew rapidly in size in the first half of the 19th century and attracted ever greater numbers of ships, through the 1860s there were simply too many dock facilities competing for trade, and towards the end of the century nearly all the dock companies were in serious financial difficulty.

The 20th Century

By 1900 the situation had deteriorated to such an extent that the Government was forced to intervene and establish a Royal Commission to study the management of the docks. After years of hot debate, the Bill that led to the creation of the Port of London Authority (PLA) was introduced by David Lloyd George (Liberal) in April 1908 as one of his final acts as President of the Board of Trade. The task of guiding it through the House of Commons fell to his successor, Winston Churchill, at that time a Liberal too. The Bill received Royal Assent in December 1908. The Commission identified poor management as the core problem and in 1909 the Government in effect nationalised the docks (an unprecedented step at this time, nearly 40 years before the wave of nationalisation introduced by Attlee's Labour Government in the late 1940s).

The new PLA began an immediate programme of modernisation, dredging a deeper channel in the river and constructing the King George V Dock.

The outbreak of World War I brought complete confusion to the dock and shipping industries. The Government requisitioned materials, ships and road and rail transport as well as diverting labour.

Overall trade continued as usual although essentials, and not luxuries, were predominant. In fact, with Antwerp and Rotterdam out of use, the port initially benefited. The war was conducted mostly without air attack by either side, the only impact being that of the German U-boat campaign in 1917. This successfully discouraged shipping from using London for fear of attack and briefly interrupted trade movement. The port experienced minimal damage during these years and by the end of the war it was relatively easy to return to its continuing development, remaining the world's greatest port during the 1920s and 1930s.

The PLA had had an inspiring period of reconstruction but events, such as the industry's paralysing General Strike of 1926 and the Wall Street Crash, were beginning to affect Britain and other nations.

The result was Britain failed to recover its place as the foremost manufacturing county in the world. This in turn impacted on sea carriage, docks and trade.

However the general trade of the port flourished with development continuing.

With the outbreak of the World War II imminent, the Government needed to ensure the continuation of essential port services. At their request a scheme for the wartime administration of the port was drawn up with other defensive measures being implemented during 1938–39. A civil defence scheme, which included the creation of a River Emergency Service, was

RMS Rangitiki *is seen berthed at Number 29 Shed, Royal Albert Dock, in the 1950s.*

planned and the necessary training of key men took place, with equipment purchased and stored in readiness.

With the outbreak of the war on 2 September 1939 the Royal Navy established guard ships, batteries were manned on both banks of the lower river and in the middle of the reaches in the dock and, in industrial areas, barrage balloons were inflated.

Everyone was aware that at some point the River Thames would become a target. Passive defences in the port were ready with stringent security measures in place enforced by the PLA's own police at the docks and by the Thames Division of the Metropolitan Police in the river.

It was during November 1939 that the first German bomb fell on the Thames Estuary and throughout the war this area was heavily targeted. The first significant attack on London came, however, on 7 September 1940 when 375 enemy planes struck at the Thames and its docks. For 57 consecutive nights the tideway was under near continual attack with transport, communications, sheds and warehouses destroyed or damaged.

V1 rocket damage in the Royal Victoria Dock, 1944.

The river came into its own during this period, being used as the main highway into London as it was never disrupted by bomb debris, craters or fire. A service of tugs and launches was provided by the Port Emergency Committee on behalf of the London Passenger Transport Board.

During the first attack the docks and East London were set ablaze, 436 Londoners were killed and another 1,600 were badly injured. Many raids were to follow, mostly by night but the Blitz on London was ultimately unsuccessful. London literally soldiered on.

At the end of 1941 London's shipping traffic had been reduced to about one quarter of its usual volume, with much of the normal shipping traffic diverted to emergency anchorages in the Clyde. By 1944 war supplies were pouring into the port in large quantities and both before and after D-Day traffic flowed almost without stopping into and out of dock premises.

Marshalling for D-Day began in London on 27 May and in Tilbury on 28 May. Never before had the Thames seen such a fleet of armed merchantmen and ships of war. One of the most technically significant moments in port history took place as a steady flow of deep sea ships, coasters, tugs, barges, oilers and landing craft joined in the estuary. On 6 June the fleet was ready and the D-day armada set sail with 307 ships from London carrying some 50,000 servicemen, nearly 80,000 tons of military supplies and about 9,000 vehicles.

Bombing of the port still continued. The enemy had introduced the pilotless plane and the rocket bomb which targeted the Docklands area, causing high casualties and damage.

Following the war the Port was now in a worse state than it had been since the beginning of the century. Nearly 900 missiles, as well as thousands of incendiary bombs, had fallen on PLA property as well as numerous attacks on private riverside property. The most damaging aspect at that time was the loss of some 50% of the total storage accommodation.

Wartime reconstruction of the Thames was completed by 1950. The PLA now realised that long-term planning was essential for development of the port and to keep ahead of the demands made upon its services. The nature of the business was such that these requirements could change at any time with revolutionary developments forcing dock operators to modify or completely alter their plans.

The Port of London was approaching its best year in 1964 when trade exceeded 61 million tonnes and the number of enclosed docks reached its peak. However, it was a short-term boost.

With the advent of the container system and other advances in technology London, as an up river port, had no real future. The bulk cargo ships could be offloaded in 36 hours with little human handling. Previously it had taken three weeks. Stevedores (dockworkers) became part of history and the mighty new freighters were unable to pass through the locks. The number of workers and vessels needed in the port decreased dramatically. One by one the docks closed with the three Royal Docks being the last to cease commercial operation in 1981. The trade unions failed to recognise what was happening. They were still back in the 1930s. Strikes were not going to change the march of progress.

As Tilbury developed the enclosed docks were steadily shut and eventually turned over to developers along with the riverside warehouses with most of them gone by 1981. The East India, London, Surrey and St Katharine Docks closed in the late 1960s and early 1970s. Between 1980 and 1983 the West India, Millwall and the Royal Docks were also shut.

Now the runway. The King George V Dock in the 1960s.

Tilbury was privatised in 1992. The PLA exists today but does not own any docks and plays an entirely different role. The PLA acts mainly as a managing authority for the tidal stretch of the River Thames, ensuring safe navigation, and the well-being of the port and its activities. It has a number of statutory duties, including river traffic control, security, navigational safety (including buoys, beacons, bridge lights and channel surveys), conservation (dredging and maintaining certain river banks), encouraging both commercial and leisure uses of the river, and protecting its environment. It is not responsible for the Thames Barrier which is managed by the Environment Agency in its flood management role.

The whole area, covering nearly nine square miles had become derelict and after much discussion the London Docklands Development Corporation (LDDC) was created in 1981 with the aim of regenerating the complex and largely water-fronted expanse of land.

London did not know it, but was ready for something special. The catalyst for London City Airport had been set.

Chapter Three
The London Docklands Development Corporation (LDDC)

It came – it did – and it went gracefully

In May 1979 following 'The winter of discontent', James Callaghan's Labour Government collapsed, the result of a no confidence vote in the House of Commons.

The Conservatives, led by Margaret Thatcher, took over. Britain was in decline. The 'swinging sixties' had become the 1970s, the age of the Austin Allegro, a forgotten car.

With the new Cabinet Michael Heseltine was appointed Secretary of State for the Environment, fully understanding the needs of a country ready for rejuvenation.

With his publishing background he was not a typical career politician. Carrying a flowing mane he somehow symbolised 'action man' when it came to newspaper headlines.

The revitalisation of Liverpool is a shining example of Heseltine's efforts, but his decision to create the London Docklands Development Corporation (LDDC) is not so well known. Mr Heseltine, as he was then, saw the task not only to create jobs but to regenerate the land, turning decaying 'brown field sites' into prosperous developments.

He described what he saw in his book *Life in the Jungle*, a minor classic in its time taking in the events as he came into power.

'I had found myself in a small plane, heading in that direction by way of the London's East End. My indignation at what was happening on the South Bank was as nothing compared to my reaction to the immense tracts of dereliction I now observed. The rotting docks – long since abandoned for deep-water harbours downstream able to take modern container ships – the crumbling infrastructure that had once supported their thriving industry and vast expanses of polluted land left behind by modern technology and enhanced environmentalism. The place was a tip: 6,000 acres of forgotten wasteland.'

Between 1978 and 1983 over 12,000 jobs were lost in the area. The transport infrastructure was very poor. The extent of dereliction was so high that the cost of rebuilding was completely beyond the means of most developers and investors.

With this in mind the LDDC was established in 1981. Appointed as Chief Executive was Reg Ward, a one-time tax inspector but steeped in the politics of local government, a former Chief Executive of the London Borough of Hammersmith and Fulham, and later of Hereford and Worcester County Council.

Ward's appointment was inspired, although not appreciated by everyone at the time. He fought and beat Ken Livingstone, Leader of the Greater London Council (GLC), who was opposed to the airport and later had to eat humble pie, officially opening the Docklands Light Railway (DLR) extension just before Christmas 2005.

On at least one occasion, for example, Ward dodged phone calls from a secretary of state for several days, knowing that if they spoke one of his road schemes would be blocked. While Michael Heseltine was a great admirer of his gung-ho approach (as, apparently, was Prince Philip), Nicholas Ridley, who became Environment Secretary in 1986, was less enthusiastic.

In itself the LDDC had very little money, but it was given three main powers to deliver regeneration. The first was to acquire land – compulsorily if need be. This meant that it could enter into commercial deals with developers. Secondly, and controversially, it took planning powers, but not powers of planning public services, away from local authorities. This meant, for example, that it could react quickly with outline planning permission, typified by Canary Wharf. And finally the LDDC had the powers and resources to provide new or refurbish existing infrastructure, such as the DLR. Additionally, the Government set up an Enterprise Zone covering the Docklands.

It became clear that the demand for large industrial sites in London was no longer required – cheaper land and labour were available in Manchester and Liverpool and other British cities. Therefore the LDDC began to focus on the fact that the Docklands was close to the City of London and this made the area a good site for secondary office location. 'Too close' was the call from The Square Mile worried that its dominance of the banking scene was to be eroded. In fact the City of London was running out of space and today the two centres work hand in hand.

In the first years of its life the LDDC oversaw several office and apartment building schemes built on Heron Quays and Surrey Quays as well as riverside accommodation. The headquarters was the redundant Dockmasters House and for entertaining prospective investors a catering barge was moored just across the road. Its most speculator success was the construction of Canary Wharf, controversial at the time, and to have an extraordinary future story line in itself.

Canary Wharf, the name usually given to the whole complex, contains around 16,000,000 square feet of office and retail space, of which around 7,900,000 square feet is owned by Canary Wharf Group. Something in the order of 100,000 plus people work in the complex today and it is home to the world or European headquarters of numerous major banks, professional services firms and media organisations including Barclays, Citigroup, Clifford Chance, Credit Suisse, EY, Fitch Ratings, HSBC, Infosys, J. P. Morgan, KPMG, MetLife, Moody's, Morgan Stanley, RBC, S&P Global, Skadden, State Street, Mirror Newspaper and Thomson Reuters.

The project was conceived by Canadian company Olympia & York, controlled by Paul Reichmann, a refugee from Nazi Austria. Reichmann may have masterminded one of the world's great commercial developments but preferred a modest lifestyle.

Construction began in 1988, and the first buildings were completed in 1991, including One Canada Square, which became the UK's tallest building at the time and a symbol of the regeneration of Docklands. By the time it opened, the London commercial property market had collapsed, and Olympia & York Canary Wharf Ltd filed for bankruptcy in May 1992.

In December 1995 an international consortium, backed by the former owners of Olympia & York and other investors, bought the scheme. The new company was called Canary Wharf Ltd, and later became Canary Wharf Group.

In July 2014 Canary Wharf Group was granted planning permission for a major eastwards expansion of the Canary Wharf estate including shops, 1.9 million square feet of commercial offices and 3,100 homes with the first buildings to be occupied at the end of 2018.

Canary Wharf had its problems but was not the only project to venture into receivership, the most spectacular being Lehman Brothers, the tenants of 25 Bank Street, Heron Quays. Facilities included a television broadcast studio, meeting rooms and a 400-seat auditorium, massive data centre, four trading floors, 20 office floors, a gym and fitness centre and staff restaurant. Lehman brothers collapsed in September 2008.

The LDDC created a cheap rail scheme, the DLR, run with driverless trains and costing only £77 million. The DLR arrived in 1987 and the Jubilee Line in 1999. This in turn made the whole area more accessible to the public and helped create the conditions for further development. The derelict Custom House area became ExCeL London which in turn led to the development of hotels and other services in the area. By car it was less than five minutes from London City Airport. It was also linked by the North London Line from Custom House station to Silvertown for London City Airport station, which closed in 2008

The Ledger Building was for some time the headquarters of the LDDC. It is now a Wetherspoons.

to make way for Crossrail. By that time the LDDC was history.

During the 1980s private housing developed – at first it was an opportunity for those working in the area to buy property cheaply – on many of the developments local council tenants were given first opportunities to buy at discounted prices. Then again in the later 1990s London had a huge house price boom bringing the middle classes to the area which in turn encouraged shops, restaurants and bars. All in all during the years of the LDDC operation £1.86 billion was invested by the public sector, £7.7 billion by the private sector, 25 million square feet of industrial space was built along with 24,046 homes and 95,000 jobs.

With no planning permission required in the manner we know now, speed of construction was astonishing, almost anything could go ahead with the result that there were many varied designs, styles and layouts. Today the buildings look like they were developed over a period, but in fact were all completed over a very short timescale.

Some will disagree but it worked. And many of the original warehouses still stand, some transformed into small workshops, others bars and restaurants. Not everything was pulled down. Restraint was available if the LDDC thought necessary.

There were vociferous complaints from the local community about the LDDC, arguing that they were not satisfactorily consulted over the Docklands development and that the jobs created from the various schemes were not ones that matched the skills of the residents. The new populace were in fact economic migrants drawn to what was increasingly being seen as a revitalised area and the place to seriously consider for office space. Without these new people, the area would have never expanded such as it did. In addition, the amount of social housing in the area is now much higher than had it been left for a local borough to develop.

The Canary Wharf shopping complex comprises of 300 shops, cafés, bars and restaurants. There is an Everyman Cinema, slightly up-market, where you can be served a meal in your armchair seat before the programme begins and plenty of gardens and patio areas to sit outside and relax on a nice day. Water surrounds you. It is a lively and attractive multifunctional venue typified by the East Wintergarden, the main hall capable of seating 500 for dinner. The place buzzes.

According to the *Daily Telegraph*: 'Ward's greatest achievement was to persuade hard-nosed City and property investors that Docklands revival was going to work. By 1986, the LDDC had spent around £300 million of public money, but had succeeded in attracting £1.4 billion in private investment.'

His forthright style did not sit well with his colleagues in central government. Ward's disregard for Civil Service protocol and rules caused one colleague to remark: 'The corns he has stepped on would fill more shoes than even Imelda Marcos possessed.' He was eased out of the LDDC in 1988 and was never given even a minor honour for what he had achieved, but he was certainly the Lord of the Manor of Docklands, which few would dispute.

Reg Ward had learnt to fly when doing National Service with the Royal Air Force. Perhaps it was that experience that kindled the inspiration for London City Airport.

The LDDC was not set up as a permanent organisation and with its task of development by then successfully achieved it began a staged withdrawal in 1994 and was formally wound up on 31 March 1998.

Chapter Four
A Short History of Brymon Airways

25 years from start to finish

During its 25-year life Brymon Airways, based at Plymouth City Airport, was one of the most innovative of small British airlines. It opened up Plymouth for scheduled air services, flew to the most northerly airport in the British Isles, and was the airline responsible for the UK introduction of three de Havilland Canada types – the Twin Otter (DH6), a utility 20-seater; the Dash 7, a short take-off and landing (STOL) 50-passenger aircraft; and the Dash 8, 35 seats originally, and now as the Q400 able to carry up to 80 in its 2+2 cabin.

In 1981 Brymon took part in trials to consider using a short cross runway at Heathrow, but what brought it to national attention was ITN's *News at Ten*, Sunday 27 June 1982 'And Finally' segment which showed a large passenger aircraft landing in the middle of the London docks. Peter Sissons, the newsreader, was clearly intrigued. And as they say 'The rest is history!'

Brymon Aviation Ltd was incorporated on 26 January 1970, its name derived from its creators' surnames, Bryce and Amon. Bill Bryce

Bill Bryce is interviewed by Thames Television at the time of the Public Inquiry test landing at Heron Quays.

Bill Bryce (right) is seen here with fellow New Zealander, Ferrari number one Chris Amon.

was a New Zealander, who had followed his mates Chris Amon and Denny Hulme to Europe to try and establish themselves in the world of Formula One motor racing. Hulme became F1 World Champion in 1967 whilst Chris Amon was Ferrari number one 1967–69, three seasons, not actually winning a world championship race. Bruce McLaren, another kiwi, had a similar background and was the founder of the company that bears his name which is still around today making some of the world's most advanced road going cars. Sadly McLaren himself was killed at Goodwood on 2 June 1970 aged 32 when the Can-Am car he was testing crashed. Bryce fancied himself as a racing driver but found himself as a journalist reporting back home on his three more illustrious friends.

It was as an aviation entrepreneur that Bryce was to make his name, unconventional and charismatic, a man for a particular time, and not for the rules and regulations of air transport then or today.

Brymon Aviation initially operated a Cessna dealership at Fairoaks and Southampton as well as a flying school and an air taxi operation. In 1972 as Brymon Airways it began flying a nine-seat Britten-Norman Islander between RAF St Mawgan, now Newquay-Cornwall Airport, and the Isles of Scilly. Another Islander was acquired and in 1973 Bryce moved the airline's base to Roborough Airport, Plymouth, then little more than a grass field with a portacabin for an office.

Brymon quickly built up a network of routes from its bases at Plymouth and Newquay and in 1984 introduced the first DHC Twin Otter on the British aircraft register. It was a brave step. The airline was eventually to operate eight aircraft of this type.

With the introduction of Gatwick, Plymouth's first air link to London, the tiny Canadian-built Twin Otters mixed in with Virgin Atlantic's Boeing 747s and other large aircraft. In those days the 'Twotters' were single crew, just a pilot. The spare seat up front was for a passenger to use. If you were not nervous, sitting on the flight deck on the Gatwick approach was great fun. Downwind at low level you could see all that was going on.

A chance meeting between Bryce and British Midland Airways boss Michael Bishop (now Lord Glendonbrook) in September 1976 led to an important change. A discussion between the two men about BMA's Heathrow service to Newquay resulted in the sale of the complete operation, including a Dart Herald aircraft and route licence, for £100,000.

Brymon had reached the big time and on a

Veteran Fleet Air Arm and Korean War pilot Captain Harry Gee led Brymon Airways' technical team on the development of London City Airport.

Brymon called its cabin service on the Dash 7 CITYCLASS but in fact it was economy.

Friday sometimes operated three return services between Terminal 1 and St Mawgan.

Bryce flew on the brand new de Havilland Dash 7 at Farnborough in September 1978 and was impressed. He saw it as the answer to Plymouth Airport's communication problems with London. The railway service was poor, the alternative was a 200-mile road journey. With a proper concrete runway and the new aircraft the city and Brymon could literally take-off.

Financing such a project, and the introduction of a technically advanced aircraft, could have been a step too far for the airline.

All was not lost. But they were lucky.

The Chevron Oil consortium was seeking a way of cutting the cost of moving staff from Aberdeen to its North Sea rigs in the Unst field. The answer was Dash 7 to Unst, Britain's most northerly airport, and then by Bristow Sikorsky S-61N helicopters for the final 65-mile leg to the platform.

Bryce put in a bid, rumoured to be worked out on the back of an envelope and, rather typical of the man, winning the crucial contract.

Brymon Airways took on four Dash 7s, two to be based at Aberdeen, but also a pair at Plymouth. Bryce personally got involved with the building of the runway at what at last was Plymouth City Airport. A tractor operator became another of his skills. Operating a converted milk float for baggage handling was also an occasional occurrence.

A new terminal building was erected. Often Bryce could be seen late in the afternoon jumping on his motorcycle and belting off to Newquay to catch the evening Heathrow flight. Bill lived on the very up-market St Georges Hill estate, Weybridge, next door to comedian Dick Emery. The pair were often seen at the weekend burning up the local lanes on their bikes.

In 1981 the Dash 7s arrived and with these popular aircraft the services from Plymouth to Heathrow via Newquay and then back to Plymouth flourished.

The last flight of the day, the fourth rotation, routed back from London via the Cornish airport. Plymouth boomed and so seemingly did

Coffee and biscuits were served on the LCY waterbus service.

the airport. But it was all superficial. Bryce had overreached himself.

Gloria Hunniford tried the service to Paris in the very early days, flying to Charles de Gaulle airport and back in the morning with plenty of time to spare for her 14:00 BBC Radio show from Broadcasting House.

By summer 1983 Brymon Airways was in serious financial trouble, yet was the lead carrier for the proposed STOLPORT in the London docks. If Brymon collapsed the whole scheme could be in mortal danger.

Mindful of the fact that with the proposed new airport there could be more aircraft sales, de Havilland Canada took a controlling interest in the carrier. Tom Appleton, the chief Dash 7 development pilot and by then a senior executive, became Chairman of Brymon Airways, albeit on a temporary basis.

By chance, a resident not that far from Plymouth was Charles Stuart, a former British Airways director, and the exact opposite of Bryce, tall and urbane, softly spoken and very British, unlike the sometimes brash New Zealander. He also knew his way around the airlines of Europe and was media friendly. He quickly established himself amongst the Plymouth elite sitting on various boards and very much supporting the city in its drive to attract business investment.

Stuart quickly gained the support of his former colleague, the then Colin Marshall (later Lord) CEO of British Airways, when he asked for a half million pound cash injection, possibly the best money BA has ever spent. The pair of five Brymon landing slots at Heathrow that BA were eventually to acquire are worth tens of millions today.

On 1 January 1986, six senior Brymon Airways executives, led by CEO Charles Stuart, with assistance from BA, and collectively known as the Plimsoll Line Ltd, purchased the carrier from de Havilland Canada with British Airways taking a 40% interest. By now it also owned a very long lease on Plymouth City Airport.

Charles Stuart preached the virtues of London City Airport during what might be called its pregnancy and birth. He was a fine doctor for the project working well with Mowlem and the LDDC team under Reg Ward.

Stuart's wife Anne had been a pupil at the City of London School for Girls. She had taken a keen interest in the venture which had a working name of STOLPORT. It was during a sixth form group visit to what was then a building site that the name London City Airport was suggested, and it clicked. Mowlem to their credit agreed. The new airport had a proper name.

Visitors inspect the Dash 7 at Heron Quays June 1983.

When Brymon Airways first came to Heathrow from Newquay in January 1977 it flew an ex-British Midland Dart Herald.

Charles Stuart, Brymon Chief Executive, welcoming the Queen at Plymouth City Airport.

In October 1992, Brymon Airways merged with Birmingham European Airways to form Brymon European Airways. This was bought jointly by British Airways and Maersk Air, in 1993. British Airways fully acquired Brymon Airways, whilst Maersk Air purchased the Birmingham European Airways section. Charles Stuart retired and the new management cancelled the London City operation citing losses. British Airways found more profitable uses for the five Brymon Heathrow slots, Brymon only using Gatwick for its London and airline connecting traffic. It was the steal of the century.

BA sold Plymouth City Airport to a local property developer, Sutton Harbour Holdings Plc, who created a new airline, Air Southwest, at the airport using some of the Brymon management team. The carrier folded in 2011. Today the airport itself lies moribund, Sutton Harbour is keen to build houses, whilst a group called Fly Plymouth has serious plans for its reopening.

Bill Bryce returned to New Zealand and died in 2003. Charles Stuart passed away aged 64 in 1993.

Dash 7 G-BRYA of Brymon Airways getting airborne at Plymouth City Airport.

Chapter Five
London City Airways (Eurocity Express)

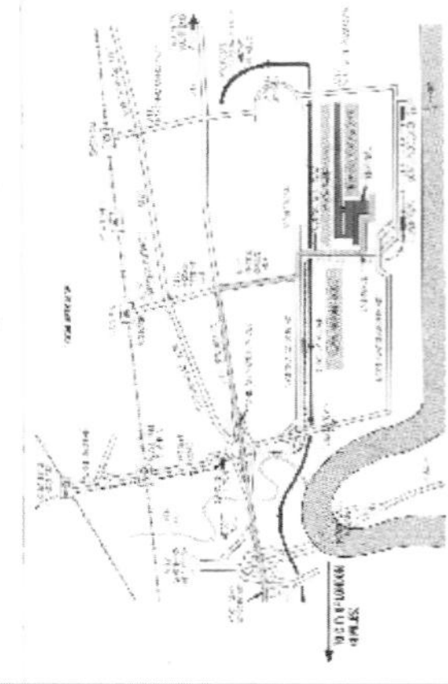

HOW TO GET TO LONDON CITY AIRPORT

BY TAXI: From the Bank of England, journey is approximately 6.7 miles. From the rank at Plaistow Underground (District Line) approximately 2 miles.

BY ROAD: From the City (Aldgate) take the A13 Commercial Road. Pass Blackwall Tunnel and Canning Town flyover then turn right into A112 (Prince Regent Lane). Turn left at the bottom, onto Connaught Road. The Airport entrance is on the left.

BY COACH: Green Line service No. 787 'London City Express' every 20 minutes throughout the day from Victoria via Embankment, Blackfriars, Cannon Street, Aldgate and All ... the DLR station Isle of Dogs. Check with reservations for full schedule.

BY RAIL: The terminal is 300 yards from Silvertown Station on the North London link. This connects to the underground at West Ham (District Line) and Stratford (Central Line). ... to Silvertown is only eight stations with one change at Stratford.

IN-FLIGHT SERVICE

Meals appropriate to the time of day are available on all flights, along with a complimentary bar, newspapers and magazines.

Whatever the time of day we hope that the meal provided will be enjoyable and a few more time for that important meeting on arrival.

Bon appetit.

DAYS OF OPERATION

1 — Monday
2 — Tuesday
3 — Wednesday
4 — Thursday
5 — Friday
6 — Saturday
7 — Sunday

All services are operated with De Havilland Dash 7 aircraft. The aircraft seat 44 in a Business Class configuration offering 32 inch seat pitch, which equals the highest industry standards. A large hanging wardrobe and spacious overhead lockers provide ample accommodation for hand baggage, providing even greater time savings for the busy executive. However, if you are carrying baggage for a longer stay, a generous baggage allowance of 30 kilos is available to each passenger. It should be noted that the interior of the aircraft may vary.

Bob Schumacher, today United Airlines' Managing Director UK and Ireland, was at London City Airport from the beginning and says that there was a real excitement across the Eurocity team – assembled from British Midland Airways' (BMA) old hands, flight deck and technical crew in the main, as the build-up to the airport and the opening of its doors. Later he was to join Continental Airlines at Gatwick and head up the move to Heathrow and amalgamation with United. Here he recollects exciting times at Eurocity Express.

'The airport brought a transport revolution – and a local fascination to a part of London whose connectivity with foreign shores had been solely limited to seaborne traffic through the London docks. There were also employment opportunities in what was, at the time, a deprived part of East London. Fire officers doubled-up as baggage loaders and airfield operatives as the airport became fully functional.

London City Airport was revolutionary in bringing a STOL (short take-off and landing) airport right into the heart of Europe's largest capital city. It was equally ahead of its day both in terms of the infrastructure – or lack thereof, and the redevelopment of the local area. Canary Wharf was, at that time, the eastern edge of urban redevelopment and the immediate vicinity was semi-derelict and unattractive. How different to today!'

Created in 1964 and headed by Michael Bishop (now Lord Glendonbrook) British Midland Airways (BMA and later bmi) had always been a thorn in the side of British Airways (BA) and its predecessors. BA itself had been fashioned as a State enterprise in 1974. It was the amalgamation of British European Airways (BEA) and the British Overseas Airways Corporation (BOAC).

Same owner, British Midland, same aircraft – Dash 7 G-BOAX – but seen on its first Eurocity Express landing in 1987 (below left) and in London City Airways livery (above).

With headquarters at the palatial Donington Hall near East Midlands Airport, BMA was thought of as a Midlands airline, but in fact Bishop, Manchester born, had been educated at the prestigious Mill Hill School in North London. Keen on aviation from a very young age he had joined the embryo airline from its beginnings rising to General Manager in 1969 and Managing Director in 1972. He was active with the London-based d'Oyly Carte Opera Company, which he chaired, and was a sometime resident of London's Savoy Hotel. He has always been a keen non-resident Londoner.

In a strange twist of fate it was in 1977 that Michael Bishop sold Bill Bryce of Brymon a Handley Page Dart Herald aircraft for use on the Newquay – Heathrow route signalling that airline's rise to prominence.

Bishop had always been a man of vision. He was later to lead attempts to renegotiate the UK – USA bilateral known as Bermuda 2, his success being overtaken by the EU – US Open Skies Agreement 2010.

Bishop saw London City Airport as the sort of innovation he wanted to get involved with and, perhaps, to cross swords again with Charles Stuart, his adversary at British Airways during the early 1980s.

Eurocity Express was incorporated in 1986 and purchased two Dash 7s. It entered into a bid to secure a partnership with Air France, but lost out to Stuart and Brymon. It was to later take the last Dash 7 ever built.

With Air France failing to come on board for Eurocity Express it was always going to be a struggle to compete in the Paris market. A codeshare with the Belgian airline Sabena saw greater success on the London City – Brussels route.

In its early days London City Airport was difficult to get to by public transport or driving. No easy drive from the A13 and A406 (North Circular Road) at the time then, a poor local bus service, and whilst the North London Line Silvertown Station had 'for London City Airport' added to its name, it was little used.

Today the North London Line rail infrastructure is the core of Crossrail (Elizabeth Line) and the line itself has been transformed into the highly successful London Overground.

What was popular, but expensive to operate, was a water bus service from Embankment, stopping at nearby Blackfriars Station and disembarking its passengers at a wharf just upstream from the Thames Barrier. It was then a five-minute coach transfer to the airport. Brymon promoted it actively, Eurocity Express just tagged along. Its limitations were the weather. As soon as any kind of winds blew across the

Thames services were cancelled. This kind of river connectivity, so prevalent today, was to some extent 'ahead of its time'.

Operations began with the opening of the airport with flights to Brussels and Paris. Amsterdam was added in 1988. A summer schedule to Jersey and weekend ad hoc charters came along later.

Brymon's decision to close the Paris route for alleged air traffic safety reasons just before Christmas 1987 affected both airlines. Into 1988 flights used to come and go with just a handful of passengers. Losses mounted quickly but Bishop was confident that the airport would work.

Later that year the airline was renamed as London City Airways so as to identify more closely with its base. Orders were placed for three more de Havilland Canada Dash 7s, the final production airframes of this type. The two original planes were sold when a third aircraft arrived but in 1988 a further Dash 7 was purchased from Maersk Air to increase the fleet to four.

Without the Air France contract, and no continental gateway airline interested in a partnership, London City Airways was doomed to fail, closing in 1990 following sustained financial losses. The aircraft were transferred to the parent British Midland Airways.

Bob Schumacher said: 'The airline industry is always full of innovation and ideas – and this was one ambitious experiment in its time. It was a slow-burn but no one can deny its success today. One might therefore argue that BMA capitulated too quickly. Brymon was to follow and is also no longer with us. But without London City Airport would Canary Wharf be as prominent and successful as it is today? We will never know the answer to that but I am proud to have been there at the very beginning!'

Michael Bishop, Chairman of Eurocity Express, LCY Chairman Philip Beck and the Queen, on the occasion of the terminal opening.

CHAPTER SIX
THE DOCKLANDS LIGHT RAILWAY

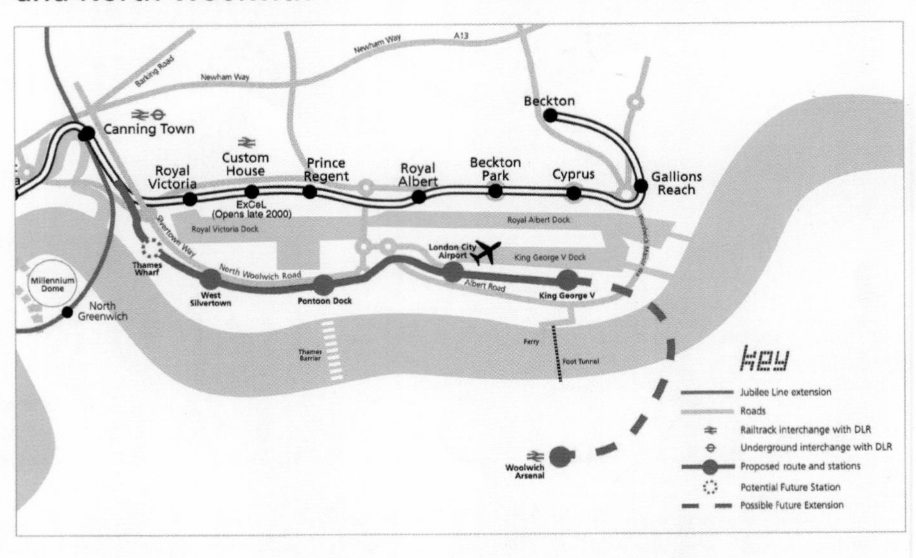

In 2009 the final DLR extension was completed to Woolwich Arsenal.

Nearly two-thirds of London City Airport passengers arrive and depart by the DLR, mostly via the Canning Town Underground/Jubilee Line intersection, but an increasing number use Woolwich Arsenal, on the southern side of the River Thames with its links to the South-East and Kent.

The DLR was a long time in its making. While the track itself is new, much of the infrastructure is built on Victorian viaducts which are well over 100 years old.

During the second half of the 19th century a proliferation of railway lines developed in the east of London mainly to support the ever-expanding Docklands, and giving connections to a much wider hinterland to the north. The poorly built roads were the province of single riders on horses, or carriages of varying standards, for both passengers and goods. The coal-fired trains might have been smelly, but were a major improvement on the reeking roadways.

Originally called the Commercial Railway, and dating from 1840, the line which developed into the London and Blackwell Railway became the main service provider in the area, running from the Tower of London area to North Greenwich and also to the southern tip of the Isle of Dogs. It finally closed in 1966 due to lack of traffic but its legacy lives on. Take the DLR from Tower Gateway to Poplar and you will see the remains of many abandoned sidings and branch lines long given up.

Over the next 15 years various schemes were suggested to resurrect the old track, build a tramway, or even extend the London Underground. It was recognised that a mass people mover was a crucial requirement for any redevelopment to succeed in East London. People had to get to and from work cheaply, and with a reliable service.

Until the coming of the London Docklands Development Corporation (LDDC) in 1981 there was no clear direction with both central and local government having different ideas. A need for a transport carrier was not in question – budgetary concerns being the major reason for a lack of action. No scheme ever got off the ground.

With the inauguration of the LDDC times changed. Public transport development was a priority if it were to succeed. The then London Transport (Transport for London – TfL – was a Ken Livingstone idea from 2000) was asked to evaluate a number of plans to develop a light railway system connecting the Docklands to Central London. It did seem a sensible solution, with much of the permanent way still in existence and expensive tunnelling not required. The official cost for stage one was just £77 million (£215 million at 2017 prices), remarkably cheap even by the standards of the day.

The chosen system, constructed by a consortium called GEC Mowlem, consisted of two routes; Stratford to Island Gardens on the Thames, and Tower Gateway to Island Gardens, connecting at West India Quay and then south through the Isle of Dogs via the developing Canary Wharf. The Greenwich Foot Tunnel, opened in 1902, still connects to the Cutty Sark, across the river in its Greenwich dry dock.

There is a train at least every 10 minutes to Bank taking 22 minutes.

From the north bank of the Thames there are notable views to the classical buildings of the former Greenwich Hospital and the National Maritime Museum, with Greenwich Park forming a backdrop. The track was further extended under the Thames to Greenwich itself and finally Lewisham, where it connects with National Rail, and completed in December 1999. There are plans for a Greenwich cruise liner terminal capable of taking ships up to 60,000 tons. At present smaller cruise ships moor in the Thames with transfer by tender.

The original route ran for eight miles (as against 24 miles now), had 15 stations and 11 trains. The units were driverless, a first for London and controlled by a computer, with input, when required, from a Train Captain. The DLR, running from both Tower Gateway and Stratford to Island Gardens, was officially opened by Queen Elizabeth on 30 July 1987.

As the Docklands area developed it quickly became apparent that the DLR had to increase capacity. Since the beginning of the line four main developments and enhancements have taken place, with plenty of further ideas originating,

mainly in respect of where to extend from Bank, north to Kings Cross, or south to The Strand area. Still no decisions have been made.

The first set of enhancements took place between 1991 and 1994. It included extending the line to Bank, doubling the trains to two units, vastly increasing the capacity of Canary Wharf station to include six platforms and integration into the malls and office towers around, and a route from Poplar to Canning Town, a vital piece of the East London light railway development.

Canning Town was the gateway to London City Airport with the next step an extension via the airport to the DLR station at King George V, opposite the easterly runway touchdown point. The airport station was built with a covered way straight into the terminal. It was high profile. Ken Livingstone, the then Mayor of London, opened the extension in December 2005, much to his chagrin, as he was opposed to the airport. Indeed, the DLR connection to London City Airport could have been part of the initial plans for the system if it was not for his total lack of interest or, some would say, unhelpfulness. Also attending the opening ceremony was Lord Coe, Chairman of the London Organising Committee of the Olympic and Paralympic Games 2012, and Colin Jackson, Olympic silver medallist and twice world champion.

At the same time a branch from Canning Town to Beckton was inaugurated including a station at Custom House on the North London Line, since that time the main transport access for ExCeL London.

With the strong backing of the Lewisham Borough Council the line was further extended in January 2009 under the Thames to Woolwich Arsenal connecting to National Rail and the Kent lines. Woolwich quickly proved profitable.

With the build-up towards the London Olympics, many of the stations were extended and three-car trains introduced. The DLR route from the airport to Stratford was a key element of the transport infrastructure for the London Olympics. The branch cost nearly twice that of the original scheme, £140 million.

The last extension, funded from the Olympic 2012 budget, was the line from Canning Town to Stratford and Stratford International with through trains starting at Woolwich and giving airport passengers direct Queen Elizabeth Park access. During the Games, the DLR carried around twice the usual average number of daily passengers, with up to 500,000 people on the busiest days. Passengers could now fly into LCY

LCY to Stratford completed well in time for the Olympics (left to right) Transport Minister Karen Buck, Colin Jackson, Lord Coe, Ken Livingstone, Denise Lewis.

Canary Wharf station is by far the busiest on the network.

from as far afield as New York and be at the Olympic centre within 30 minutes of actually touching down, a gold medal achievement.

Currently trains run westbound from London City Airport about every ten minutes to Bank, a major intersection with the Northern and Central Lines, and the non-stop service to Waterloo station. Some services go to Tower Gateway. Trains from London City Airport run every ten minutes to Stratford International (adjacent to Queen Elizabeth II Stadium). Journey time is seven minutes to Canning Town to interchange with the Beckton branch of the DLR and with the Jubilee Line; 12 minutes to the Poplar interchange for the Canary Wharf and Lewisham branch, and 22 minutes to Bank in the City of London.

Trains run eastbound every five minutes to Woolwich Arsenal.

KeolisAmey Docklands Ltd (KAD) operates the trains and stations and maintains much of the network. KAD took over the franchise from Serco Docklands Ltd in December 2014 following a competitive tendering process.

In 2016, 117 million passengers used the DLR with just over three million passing through London City Airport, making it possibly the busiest single platform station in the entire TfL network, a remarkable achievement.

The DLR does not directly connect with the new Elizabeth Line (Crossrail) except at Custom House and the Beckton extension. It is possible to link at Woolwich and Canary Wharf but a walk is involved.

Year	Number of stations	Number of passengers (millions)	Number of trains	Length (miles)
1988	15	10	11	8
1998	29	28	70	14
2006	38	64	94	19
2016	45	117	149	24

Chapter Seven
Canary Wharf

The Canary Wharf complex in 2017 looking towards LCY.

Canary Wharf, the London headquarters of many of the world's major financial institutions, professional firms and businesses, lies on the Isle of Dogs, evolving from humble origins.

It became known as the Isle of Dogs when Henry VIII's dogs were walked on it regularly during his reign at the start of the 16th century.

Until the 18th century the Isle of Dogs was mainly agricultural land on the edge of a burgeoning metropolis.

Canary Wharf, on the other hand, takes its name from the Canary Islands from where bananas were imported to the West India Docks. Charles Dickens described the Docklands in the 1860s as a place where 'accumulated scum of humanity seemed to be washed from higher grounds, like so much moral sewage'. Until the 1960s, the Isle of Dogs was, however, a hive of activity – thousands were employed on the docks and in related industries.

During the early Industrial Revolution British industry rapidly expanded, creating a huge demand for imported raw materials and the export of manufactured goods. Ship-owners and traders fought successfully for the creation of the world's first deep water enclosed docks on relatively open land east of the City, downstream of London Bridge. The West India Docks opened in 1802 and very quickly became profitable.

The introduction of containerisation and the increasingly large vessels employed to transport them required much larger wharves than London's 19th century docks could provide. Port activities moved down river to Tilbury and 75,000 direct jobs were lost in London's historic docks. Inevitably during the period from the mid-1960s to the mid-1970s, trade in the docks collapsed. The impact on the local economy was devastating. By the 1980s the site of what has become Canary Wharf lay abandoned within an area of 1,000 hectares of vacant and derelict land and docks in London's East End.

Access by road was poor and there was virtually no public transport. The Docklands area was perceived to be a dangerous wasteland of isolated council estates and abandoned buildings and docks. To the rest of London, the Docklands area was remote and difficult to reach and had little in it worth visiting. To film makers and television producers the legends of Jack the Ripper and the Kray brothers lived on. Taken together these factors proved a huge disincentive, especially to British institutional investors.

In 1981 the London Docklands Development Corporation (LDDC) was charged with the formidable task of regenerating Docklands, and key to this was a programme of enhancing the then bleak prospects of much of the area by restoring some key buildings and landscaping the most prominent derelict sites.

Much of the early debate about the area's future rightly focused on replacing the jobs lost by the closure of the docks but this proved too narrow. A response, acknowledging the past but looking to the future, was sought. However while new housing could be achieved relatively easily due to a huge pent-up demand, providing new jobs would prove problematic. In 1982 an Enterprise Zone was created on the Isle of Dogs to address this. The scheme allowed planning permission for most forms of development, subject to certain conditions and controls.

After a poor initial response, interest surged in 1983 when the first phase of the Docklands Light Railway (DLR) was announced, linking the Isle of Dogs to the edge of the City of London and investors began to realise the area's potential. Low-rise warehousing and small business units followed and although modest, this prompted wider interest. It was to open on 30 July 1987, just three months before London City Airport, passing through what is now Canary Wharf to Island Gardens.

In 1986 the deregulation of 'financial services' in the UK created a huge demand for large offices, but at that time new development in the City of London had been frustrated by extended planning inquiries.

Land in and around the West India Docks was available for development, but it was thought too remote from London's historic business centre and difficult to reach. After several aborted possibilities by potential developers and entrepreneurs the LDDC at last found a developer with true vision.

Canada's Olympia & York, headed by the Reichmann Brothers, had a track record of delivery, most notably having built The World Financial Centre in New York. It also had a highly skilled marketing and construction team seeking new opportunities.

The company's research in 1987 indicated that up to 85% of the City's office spaces were technologically obsolete and unsuited for modern requirements. Floor plates were too small and the ability to retrofit was limited.

It was not encumbered by the same prejudices about East London harboured by many in the City and it is perhaps not surprising that it was an overseas developer that had the confidence to commit to such an ambitious undertaking.

In 1988 George (today Sir George) Iacobescu came to London as Senior Vice-President of Olympia & York to oversee construction, budget and delivery of Canary Wharf. He became Chief Executive nine years later and today he remains at the helm of Canary Wharf Group.

Even though London City Airport was open, lack of access was quickly identified as one of the most significant problems that required a solution. The DLR would have to be extended to the heart of the City (Bank station) and to the airport, and plans for the Jubilee Line extension and Docklands Highways, originally proposed by the defunct Greater London Council, needed to be resurrected.

Although the Canary Wharf site, like most of the land in Docklands, was heavily polluted and had little commercial value, the LDDC demanded specific performance from Olympia & York, requiring 4.5 million square feet of development to be completed by 1991. It was Paul Reichmann's vision to create a 'total environment'.

Olympia & York wanted to create a cluster of buildings to provide critical mass. In time even the most ardent critics of tall buildings in London came to accept the spatial and aesthetic logic of Canary Wharf's cluster of 'skyscrapers'. Occupants could specify their preferred architects who, within the constraints of the Building Agreement, could ensure their client's needs were fully met. It was conceived as a mature city district with different architects commissioned for the design of each building. Every detail of the new development needed to achieve the highest standards.

Sir Roy Strong, then the Director of the Victoria and Albert Museum, was commissioned to advise on the design of Canary Wharf's squares and streets. As the strategy developed with the expansion of the estate, care was taken to endow each open space with its own distinct character; the contemplative, peaceful environment of Westferry Circus with its immaculate lawn and dense shrubbery contrasts with the hard granite paving, water fountain and sculptured ventilation drums of Cabot Square, different again to the green sward of Canada Square with its summer festivals and Christmas skating and the sylvan enclaves of Jubilee Park, ideal for sandwich lunches and summer picnics away from the hustle and bustle of daily business.

Caesar Pelli, architect of Olympia & York's World Finance Centre in New York City, was commissioned to design the centrepiece, One Canada Square, London's first modern skyscraper with 50 floors. Until the opening of The Shard it was the tallest building in London. (The Hilton Park Lane, built in 1963, only has 28 storeys.)

Olympia & York committed £100 million for the extension of the DLR to the City. The Canary Wharf DLR station was rebuilt, fully integrated into the malls below.

Despite the completion of the first phase in 1991 the institutions of the City of London were resistant to change and were reluctant to move east. Moreover, just as the first buildings were being completed in 1989 and 1990, the British economy was moving into a deep recession.

In May 1992, following difficulties with some of its North American investments and in the context of the worldwide recession, the group's UK development company, Olympia & York Canary Wharf Ltd, went into administration.

In 1993 with a working population of 7,000 people and construction of the Jubilee Line extension just beginning, a consortium of banks that were owed £500 million took over the project and succeeded in bringing it out of administration. Canary Wharf was back on track.

As the economy recovered and the much delayed construction of the Jubilee Line extension moved ahead, the fortunes of the development brightened and in 1995, Paul Reichmann, leading a group of international investors, acquired the estate once more. By 1999, with the development of the second phase complete, the working population had increased to 25,000 people and HSBC had finalised contracts for a 1.1 million square feet headquarters building. Transport infrastructure had dramatically improved with significant financial support from Canary Wharf Group. The Canary Wharf Jubilee Line station was due to open on the eve of the Millennium, and the DLR extension to Lewisham was complete. In March 1999 Canary Wharf Group Plc was floated on the London Stock Exchange to become one of the largest publicly quoted property developers in the UK.

At the turn of the century the growth of Canary Wharf was dramatic. Citigroup and Clifford Chance agreed to let significant new one million square feet of buildings and Morgan Stanley and Credit Suisse both signed leases to extend their existing occupation in new 500,000 square feet of buildings. In 2001 Lehman and Barclays Bank both agreed to lease separate one million square feet of buildings as their European and global headquarter buildings. By 2002 the working population had more than doubled to over 55,000.

In September 2008 Lehman Brothers went into administration sending an earthquake through the financial system and the banking sector in particular. At this time between 70–80% of occupiers at Canary Wharf were from the financial sector. Despite difficult market conditions, in 2010 J. P. Morgan purchased 25 Bank Street in the heart of the Canary Wharf complex, making it their European headquarters in 2012. This deal pushed the working population above 100,000 for the first time. However, as demand generally stalled, thoughts at Canary Wharf Group began to turn to the variation of the Canary Wharf tenant base.

Reflecting significant tenant diversification on the estate, agreement was reached the following year on a new 20-storey tower to be constructed at 25 Churchill Place. Initially half was let to the European Medicine Agency and subsequently the balance let to EY (Ernst and Young until 2013), the accountancy group. Canary Wharf Group had until then never undertaken residential development but in 2012 it acquired the Wood Wharf site to the east of Canary Wharf with potential for over 3,000 homes.

It was clear from the very early days that occupants of Canary Wharf would need much more than somewhere to live and work together in a pleasant and safe environment – they would want places to eat, shop and socialise. In the earliest days of development there were more market stalls than shops, and stall-holders would close early as business was so slow. As the working population started to grow so did the range of cafés, bars and restaurants, with a selection of shops providing essential services.

The necessary extension of the 'retail offer' was initially met by the 100% pre-let opening of the Canada Place Mall in 2000, anchored in 2002 by the arrival of the 100,000 square feet Waitrose Food and Home store. Today this remains the most successful store in the Waitrose group which has its best day's trading on a Saturday. Transport infrastructure at Canary Wharf has improved so that less than 5% of people working at Canary Wharf now arrive by car.

There are now over 300 shops, bars and restaurants at Canary Wharf, which includes the new Elizabeth Line station complex, and covers almost 1 million square feet. Uniquely, it is all let.

The retail offering has been complemented by an increasingly ambitious Arts and Events programme of mainly free exhibitions, concerts, performances and premier events open to visitors, residents and workers alike.

The shops, bars and restaurants of Canary Wharf attract people from a much wider area beyond the estate, across the whole of East London, and have an annual footfall of over 43 million with around 100,000 people regularly visiting at weekends. Canary Wharf is now a week-day, evening and weekend retail destination. The public art programme, which has been a feature of Canary Wharf throughout its development, has been constantly expanded and is now the largest open air corporate art collection in London, comprising around 70 pieces, all of which are available to be enjoyed free of charge by visitors to the estate.

Over the years the character of Canary Wharf has changed dramatically. Its occupants have moved from being around 20% non-financial – 80% financial to today's approximately 45% non-financial – 55% financial

Recent leasing transactions on the estate reflect this diversification with technology, media and telecommunications leasing transactions now exceeding banking and finance in number and size.

As well as Canary Wharf Group, current tenants include Bank of New York Mellon, Moody's, Euler Hermes, the Medical Defence Union and Trinity Mirror Group (*Daily Mirror, Sunday Mirror, Sunday People* and *The Wharf*).

Other tower blocks on the site embrace the one million square feet headquarter buildings occupied by HSBC, Citigroup and Barclays. A new 715,000 square feet building already partially let to Société Générale and a 60-storey residential tower called Newfoundland will also shortly be added to the changing Canary Wharf skyline.

Due to be opened in December 2018, Canary Wharf railway station on the Elizabeth Line (Crossrail) will add a direct train to Heathrow from the complex. Designed by Foster + Partners, its above-ground floors are already open with retail units, topped by a roof garden.

In 1980 there was one person employed full time at Canary Wharf – the security guard on the dock gate. Today there are more than 115,000 people working on the site which is more than in the heyday of the docks. Canary Wharf has expanded to over 16 million square feet of commercial space with ambitious plans for further growth in an additional 11 million square feet earmarked for new development.

The future of Canary Wharf is assured!

Cabot Place Mall within the Canary Wharf complex.

Chapter Eight
ExCeL London

Would ExCeL London have been built without the presence of London City Airport? It is a good and fair question. And in its turn the London Olympics of 2012 – would the site have been considered without the opening of ExCeL London in 2000?

When the bid was won in July 2005, ExCeL London and the airport were proving that there was new life to be had in East London.

By the end of the 20th century, London had a dearth of large scale exhibition and meeting centres. Earls Court, a 1930's concrete mausoleum, was too small, and in much the same area Kensington Olympia, dating from Victorian times, still only existed because it was not destroyed during World War II and was a listed structure. The three halls which make up Olympia are less than half a million square feet of cluttered space. The area around the Royal Victoria Dock remained desolate, a wasteland ripe for redevelopment.

In July 1994 the LDDC short-listed four firms to put in bids for a large-scale exhibition centre on the north side of the Royal Victoria Dock noting it was just over a mile from an international airport. By January the following year they announced that London International Exhibition Centre Ltd (LIECL) had been chosen to bring the scheme to fruition.

The idea took time to develop and finance and it was not until January 1998 that it finally got the green light. By this time a development company, Highpine Ltd, had been set up to build the centre. This was owned 68% by Malaysian financial interests and 24.5% by LIECL's shareholders. The balance of 7.5% was in the name of the LDDC, this share transferred to English Partnerships in March 1998.

The centre was constructed by Sir Robert McAlpine Ltd and opened in November 2000.

The exhibition building itself consists of two column-free, rectangular, devisable halls of approximately 479,493 square feet each, on either side of a central boulevard containing catering facilities and information points. There are also three sets of function rooms, one overlooking the water, another above the western end of the central boulevard, and the third on the north side of the building. These are used for smaller meetings, seminars, presentations, and corporate

The Connaught Bridge lies between the airport and ExCeL London.

Aerial view showing proximity of LCY at left to ExCeL London in centre.

hospitality. There are now eight hotels offering over 1,700 rooms between them, more than 30 bars and restaurants, plus 3,700 parking spaces on the campus.

One of the early problems associated with ExCeL London was the lack of quality hotel accommodation. This was alleviated in 2002 by the arrival of the first Sunborn Super Yacht Hotel. (A larger replacement Sunborn was opened in 2014 offering 130 suites, a restaurant and convention facilities.)

The centre's 'coming of age' could be considered to be 2004 when the Docklands Light Railway (DLR) opened at Custom House station (now Custom House for ExCeL) giving a direct rail service to Bank and also, via Canning Town, to the London Underground system. Previously, Custom House had been a stop on the underused North London Line.

In 2008, ExCeL London was acquired by Abu Dhabi National Exhibitions Company.

Although the Royal Victoria Dock closed to commercial traffic in 1981, it is still accessible for small ships and for the 2008 World Travel Market a 20-seat Twin Otter floatplane flew in!

On 2 April 2009, the annual G-20 Leaders' Summit on Financial Markets and the World Economy, commonly called The London Summit 2009, was held here. It was the largest gathering of world leaders London has seen since the first General Assembly of the United Nations in 1946.

The London International Convention Centre (ICC), London's first and only ICC, was opened by Mayor Boris Johnson on 20 May 2010. A self-contained complex, ICC London includes a huge, flexible, auditorium and London's largest

banqueting room, the ICC Capital Hall, which can host over 3,000 for a formal dinner. A series of conference rooms – the ICC Capital Suite – is also available, comprising 17 individual meeting rooms with the flexibility to host breakout sessions for 50 to 1,200 delegates, alongside reception and registration areas.

The eastern entrance of the facility is connected to Prince Regent station and is also served by a bus to London City Airport. This entrance to ExCeL London gives access to the International Convention Centre (ICC at ExCeL). During major shows with large visitor attendances, extra shuttle trains are run between the venue and Canning Town station, with interchange at London Underground's Jubilee Line.

For the 2012 Olympics and Paralympics ExCeL London was a key centre hosting the boxing, fencing, judo, taekwondo, table tennis,

The ExCeL London convention centre entrance.

weightlifting and wrestling. A legacy wall features hand prints of the athletes that won Gold at the venue plus the former Mayor of London Boris Johnson. On Sunday 16 December of the same year the centre played host to the BBC *Sports Personality of the Year* – the award was won by Bradley Wiggins, the Tour de France and Olympic cycling time trial champion and a Lifetime Achievement award went to Lord (Sebastian) Coe, head of the Olympic Organising Committee. 16,000 people watched at ExCeL London and 10.8 million UK television viewers.

Since June 2012, the Emirates Air Line cable car now links ExCeL London to The O2 on the Greenwich Peninsula. It was estimated to cost £60 million and 1.5 million journeys were taken on it in 2016.

ExCeL London welcomed its 20 millionth visitor on 18 June 2014.

In 2015, ExCeL London announced the opening of CentrEd at ExCeL, a dedicated training and meetings space located close to the western entrance of the venue overlooking Royal Victoria Dock, thus adding to ExCeL's wide range of flexible spaces. On offer are 29 training rooms with flexible walls to create spaces for 20 to 400 delegates.

Another water-borne hotel opened in 2016, the floating Good Hotel, originally sited in Amsterdam, it is now moored close by the Emirates Air Bridge. This unique concept offers 148 rooms, a range of meeting rooms, four-star accommodation and incorporates a social awareness business concept – its singular aim is to extensively train long-term unemployed locals in various jobs in the hospitality industry. Following successful conclusion, participants will be offered a three-month contract at Good Hotel, followed by professional mediation in the city's hotel business. The entire process gives participants a real chance to get off welfare, integrate into the economy and build themselves a new future.

ExCeL London hosts numerous industry and show business events. Just one example was the 2016 Doctor Who Celebration convention, a true carnival for the 50th anniversary of the BBC television series, *Doctor Who*.

The Virgin Active London Triathlon is held at ExCeL London on an annual basis, with the cycling and running legs taking place within and around the venue and the swimming taking place in the Royal Victoria Dock.

The Triathlon celebrated its 20th year at ExCeL London in summer 2016. It is also the organising centre for the London Marathon where 40,000 athletes checked in over three days in April 2017.

A regular feature in the ExCeL London calendar is the annual London Boat Show.

The annual World Travel Market is a major international event, much supported by London City Airport.

Highlights of the 2017 show included the boating lake, where you could try out kayaking and zorbing, talks by yachtswoman Dee Caffari and Olympic medallist Saskia Clark, the Dream Lodge Marina featuring super yachts, Marine Fashion Week catwalk and dance shows, as well as more than 300 exhibitors.

The sheer size of ExCeL London makes it ideal for the annual London Classic Car Show and Historic Motorsport International, open to the public. Hundreds of notable vehicles can be seen, and also the great racing cars of yesteryear. Just as large, rather more private, and an annual event, is DSEI, a world leading security trade fair.

ExCeL London also provides space free of charge for local schools and sports teams, in addition to hosting an annual event called 'ExCeL in the Arts' for local children to attend.

In 2018, the Elizabeth Line (Crossrail), will bring London's main line station Liverpool Street (for Stansted) to within ten minutes of ExCeL London and Tottenham Court Road only five minutes more.

Events at ExCeL London: cycle racing is an indoor event (above left), Olympic table tennis (above) and conferences (below).

Chapter Nine
The Airport Timeline

30 YEARS OF LONDON CITY

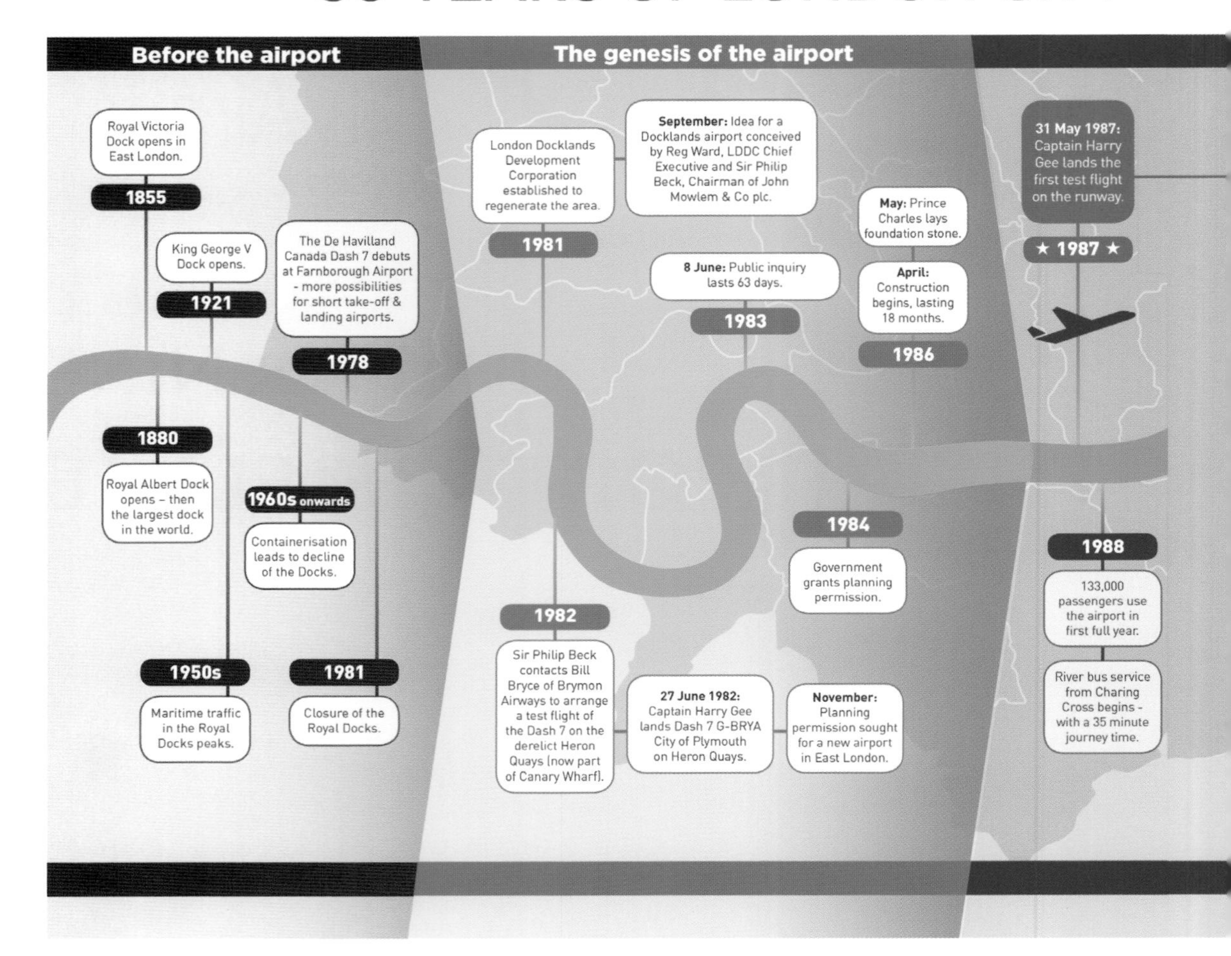

On 31 May 1987 the first ever landing took place at London City Airport.

Through the following pages the history of LCY is traced, coupled to what was going on in the outside world. Not all the routes and airlines are noted, just the most important or unusual ones, and when it comes to happenings which occurred at the time in the world we have been selective in mentioning events, personalities who have hit the headlines, major sporting occasions, and people passing on that have caught our eye and perhaps have been forgotten. You, the reader, will have your own memories and opinions and this can be challenged on the London City Airport page *www.facebook.com/londoncityair.*

Right: *The first ever landing at London City Airport.*

AIRPORT: A TIMELINE

London City Airport opens for business

26 October 1987: Inaugural commercial flights – Brymon Airways from Plymouth and Euro City Express (later London City Airways) to Paris. Brussels and Amsterdam also among first destinations.

5 November 1987: Airport is officially opened by Queen Elizabeth II.

1991
August: One Canada Square in Canary Wharf opens, then the tallest building in the UK.

1992
March: The runway is extended from 1030m to 1199m. Diana Princess of Wales opens the extension.

1995
Mowlem sells the airport for £23.5m to Irish businessman, Dermot Desmond.
9 airlines now serve 12 destinations.

1997
Airport celebrates10th anniversary and welcomes 1 million passengers in a year.

1999
Jubilee line extension opens Green Park to Stratford via Canning Town.

2000
ExCeL London and Millenium Dome (later O2 Arena) open.

2001
New arrivals hall completed.

2002
London City Airport Private Jet Centre opens.
The airport welcomes its 10 millionth passenger since 1987.

2003
New runway holding point and runway link enable 32 flights per hour.

2005
Airport gets DLR station - Docklands Light Railway extension opened by Mayor of London, Ken Livingstone.

2006
Airport acquired by Global Infrastructure Partners and AIG.

2008
£27m East Pier and apron extension project completed.
Annual passenger total reaches 3.3 million.
British Airways begins operations at London City Airport.

2009
Planning permission granted to raise number of flights to 120,000 per annum.

2012
25th anniversary and 1 millionth flight marked by a visit from The Queen.
London 2012 Olympics GB swimming team arrive at the airport to water cannon.

2014
Flybe begins operations at London City Airport.

2016
A record-breaking 4.5 million passengers use London City Airport.
£344 million development programme receives planning permission - 7 new aircraft stands, parallel taxiway and extended passenger terminal.
Airport sold to consortium of international infrastructure partners.

★ 2017 ★
30th Anniversary Year
Construction begins on the City Airport Development Programme.
£19m refurbishment of West Pier departures area.

London City Airport
30 Years
1987 - 2017

1981–1986

1981

September: The newly created London Docklands Development Corporation (LDDC) Chief Executive, Reg Ward, discussed with Philip Beck, Chairman of construction company John Mowlem & Co Plc, the idea of a heliport for Docklands.

1982

February: Mowlem contacted Brymon Airways' owner Bill Bryce, having seen a piece in *Flight International* magazine, regarding the de Havilland Canada (DHC) Dash 7 aircraft.

27 June: Brymon Airways' Chief Pilot, Captain Harry Gee, accompanied by Captain Charlie Beilby, landed a Dash 7 on Heron Quays in the West India Docks to demonstrate the feasibility of the STOLPORT (short take-off and landing) project.

Mowlem and Brymon Airways submitted to the LDDC an outline proposal for a Docklands STOLPORT city centre gateway.

August: LDDC published a feasibility study.

October: Opinion poll among residents showed two-to-one in favour of the new airport. Mowlem submitted an application for planning permission. Brymon Airways provided Dash 7 trips to Plymouth for key stakeholders, community leaders and the media to experience the quiet airliner in operation (albeit from Heathrow).

1983

Mowlem reached agreement with the Port of London Authority (PLA) to lease land in the Royal Docks.

8 June: The Public Inquiry lasting 63 days began in a former PLA office building in the Albert Basin, brought back into use for the purpose.

30 June: Captain Harry Gee returned to Heron Quays with a Dash 7 to demonstrate its quiet STOL capability to the Inspector at the Public Inquiry. Captain Richard Saw was the second person in the cockpit on this occasion.

1984

August: Secretary of State for the Environment, Patrick Jenkin, indicated that he was disposed to agree the application for outline planning permission but asked for additional work on the framing of the conditions and especially on a more easily understood system for controlling noise.

1985

March: Greater London Council (GLC) Leader, Ken Livingstone, failed in his High Court bid to secure the reopening of the Inquiry.

May: Outline planning consent was granted by the Secretary of State.

1986

February: Detailed planning consent given by LDDC.

Construction work launched by Aviation Minister, Michael Spicer.

29 May: The Prince of Wales laid the foundation stone of the terminal building.

Brymon Airways cancelled its midday flight out of Heathrow to Plymouth and Dash 7 G-BRYA made a low level pass down the King George V Dock and stole the show. (G-BRYA was the first aircraft to land at the airport in 1987.)

August: London City's first Airport Director, John Douthwaite, took up his appointment.

This was to become the apron.

Now buried under the terminal, the dry dock in 1986.

Brymon Airways Heron Quays, 1983.

Prince Charles reads the foundation stone plaque.

1986 London City prior to opening with shorter runway. Mowlem had provided for the extension.

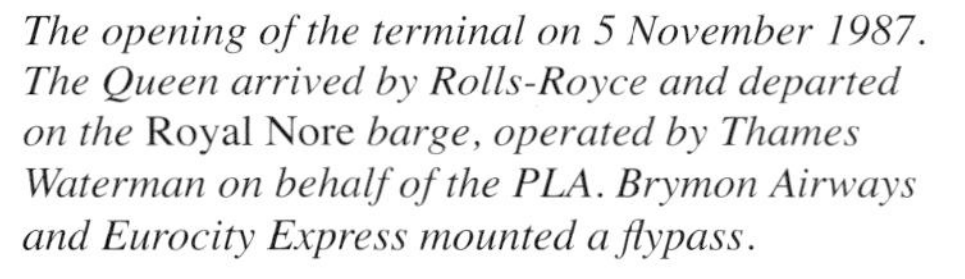

The opening of the terminal on 5 November 1987. The Queen arrived by Rolls-Royce and departed on the Royal Nore *barge, operated by Thames Waterman on behalf of the PLA. Brymon Airways and Eurocity Express mounted a flypass.*

Harvey Elliott

Harvey Elliott was born 16 April 1942. He died after a long illness 9 March 2017, aged 74. The following article published 5 November 1997 is balanced and asks all the right questions. It is a fitting tribute to a lovely man.

When Pan Am Flight 103 blew up over Lockerbie at around 19:00 on the evening of 21 December 1998 with 259 people on board, Harvey Elliott, the specialist air correspondent on *The Times,* took the lead role in producing for the following morning's edition one of the most dramatic front page stories ever.

Over the next few days he exclusively revealed the first evidence, including the discovery of heat damage on the plastic lining in one of the cargo bays, pointing to a massive bomb exploding in the hold before the airliner crashed to the ground, killing a further 11 people.

Elliott worked in Fleet Street as a reporter and specialist correspondent for 30 years, first at the *Daily Mail* and then at *The Times.* He dabbled in another career, as Press Officer for British Caledonian Airways, but two years away from the profession he loved proved too much for him and he returned to the reporting world.

A friend, who was still a reporter in the provinces, recalled a reunion after he had moved to Fleet Street when Elliott splashed out with a bottle of Meursault burgundy, costing more than his friend was earning in a week. It was very much part of Elliott's style as a Fleet Street man.

When he joined *The Times,* in September 1986, Elliott had more than proved his worth as a tough competitor in the reporting world after 18 years with the *Daily Mail* under the editorship of Sir David English, who once wrote to him: 'If I had an extra ten people like you on the staff, the *Mail* would be unstoppable.'

On the *Daily Mail* as Air Correspondent he became an authoritative chronicler of the ups and downs of Sir Freddie Laker, the private airline entrepreneur whose Laker Airways went bankrupt. Later, as Defence Correspondent, he covered the Falklands conflict in 1982 from Whitehall, writing 21 out of 24 splashes.

A lover of cricket, in the 1990s Elliott founded the Fleet Street Exiles, a mixed bag of fellow journalists and friends who could swing a bat or bowl an imperious ball, playing in the Caribbean, Australia, Sri Lanka and other exotic locations. It was a masterstroke. For one Caribbean tour he arranged for the whole team and their partners to travel between islands by cruise ship. Once, after a match in St Lucia, the players got so carried away by the beauty of the island that they returned late to the cruise ship to find a fuming captain. He had missed his departure slot and had to pay another hour's mooring fee.

Rejoining *The Times* from British Caledonian Elliott eventually combined the roles of Air Correspondent and Travel Correspondent, which provided extensive opportunities for globetrotting. It was his close contacts with the travel industry that helped him to orchestrate the sumptuous itineraries for the Fleet Street Exiles.

The London City Airport story was the culmination of an interest he took in the project since its inception, visiting the site during Ken Livingstone's High Court attempt to derail the scheme and later flying on a Dash 7 to Plymouth to interview Charles Stuart.

His article (see overleaf), published on the morning that HM The Queen opened the terminal, was accurate and as things turned out truly perceptive. He finished with the words. 'All that is needed now is an influx of passengers'. He was right but it took time!

Reproduced from THE TIMES of 5 November 1987

The slick City flyers of the future

Today the Queen opens the London City Airport, built in Docklands to serve executives requiring a swift, easy route to the Continent

Taxi drivers have not yet included it in 'the knowledge'. Much of the immediate area still resembles a bombed site. There is still confusion over the name. And only a fraction of its intended market in Europe has been opened up.

But London City Airport, or Stolport, depending on your preference, is in business.

All those involved – especially the developers Mowlem, and the airlines Brymon and Eurocity Express – believe they could be on the threshold of bringing a revolution to the way businessmen travel between London and Europe.

If they are right, the thousands working within the City of London, or within striking distance of the burgeoning East End, could be ready to turn their backs on the crowded Tube journey to Heathrow, or the battle through the backpacking holiday-makers at Gatwick, and simply take the short taxi journey to LCY, as the airport has been officially designated.

Already some doubters are predicting that the early financial analysis is, to say the least, optimistic. They claim that, even with the landing fees as high as those at Heathrow, Mowlem will find it difficult to make a return on its £30 million investment for many years. Most people, it is argued, travel on business trips from their homes rather than making spur-of-the-moment decisions to go from their offices.

So are they really likely to hail a cab, run the risk of the driver not knowing where the new airport is, fight through the heavy Docklands traffic and board a small 50-seat turbo-prop aircraft that is slower than a jet and which, on arrival in Paris or Brussels, will have no different facilities from the mass of scheduled flights coming from Heathrow or Gatwick?

Yes they will say the airlines confidently. And they also claim that, more importantly, thousands of businessmen from the Continent will want to use London City. In fact, Plymouth-based Brymon believes that at least 60 per cent of its passengers will originate in European capitals, attracted by flying to an airport within easy reach of their destination, probably the City.

Both airlines will be watching their results closely during the next few months, hoping they have even underestimated the demand and in the expectation that they will at least live up to their pre-launch publicity.

The story of the Docklands airport development is one of the almost unparalleled private optimism and enterprise. The London Docks have been at the heart of the capital's industrial life for more than 500 years. Huge ships bringing vital supplies to millions living in the South-East unloaded their cargoes on the quaysides, giving employment to thousands of dockers, shipping agents and related industries.

By the late 1970s container ships and bulk carriers had replaced the cargo carriers and despite desperate and bitter attempts by the dockers to keep them open, the London Docks were doomed.

In 1981 the up-river docks finally closed, throwing 28,000 men out of work and resulting in a gradual decay and dereliction that blighted the entire area.

But the Government decided to rejuvenate the area through the London Docklands Development Corporation, which had the power to cut through red tape and bring new industries into the 5,000 acres of wasteland. At about the same time a new breed of ultra-quiet short take-off and landing aircraft were being developed, especially in Canada, where the de Havilland Dash 7, four-engined turbo-prop was being built.

Reg Ward, head of the LDDC, saw the significance at once. He was keen to maintain some form of transport in the docks and when he began talking to Philip Beck, chairman of Mowlem, who was a private pilot and aviation enthusiast, an idea gradually began to take shape.

They contacted Bill Bryce, then the owner of Brymon, who had taken delivery of his first Dash 7, capable of carrying 50 people around 400 miles, and asked if it could land on 2,500 ft of runway. It could. The project was born.

From their first formal meeting some near miracles have been achieved in winning approval for the scheme, overcoming local opposition, proving the operation was both safe and potentially viable, building the actual airport itself and ending with an official opening by the Queen.

The slick City flyers of the future

Today the Queen opens the London City Airport, built in Docklands to serve executives requiring a swift, easy route to the Continent

Youthful look: Amanda Sayers, 28, was appointed building services manager for the venture

Basic idea is that the passenger should use it as easily as his office

Thousands will want to use the airport

Terminal covered in blue aluminium

Harvey Elliott
Air Correspondent

The airport itself lies to the east of the Isle of Dogs on 667 undeveloped acres that are larger than the City and the West End combined. Within that area a finger pier between the Albert Dock and the King George V Dock is a site tailor-made for the construction of a runway, from which the Dash 7 can operate.

Once the project was clearly on course a whole range of airlines showed an interest in flying from there and the Civil Aviation Authority began a series of route licence applications in which each had to prove its worthiness and operational capabilities.

From the six on the short list of potential operators just two now remain – Eurocity Express, a purpose-made offshoot of Michael Bishop's highly successful and slick British Midlands Airways, and Brymon, run by the former BEA boss Charles Stuart.

They will fly from land that is actually owned by Port of London Properties, originally the property division of the Port of London Authority, and leased to Mowlem, which has designed and built the airport and will operate it.

They fought through a full public inquiry, during which local objections were answered with detailed explanation, and received final planning consent in February last year.

Work on the airport itself actually began in April that year, the main concentration being on the 92-acre site itself, just north of the Thames. Working with R. Seifert & Partners as the architects and engineers Donald Butler Associates, Mowlem drew up a tight construction programme, guaranteed to complete the construction in just 18 months.

Warehouses on the site were demolished and the dock measuring 250 x 30 metres had to be decked over in an astonishing operation. The dock was dammed and drained, and 128 steel columns were built from the dock base and were capped with a giant slab of concrete that now forms the aircraft apron.

Two other dry docks were filled in to form part of the flat area at each end.

The alignment of the runway itself was dictated by a tall mill building to the west of the site and a proposed bridge over the Thames to the east. Through a trick of clever design the runway is actually two overlapping runways in one, and is fitted with the latest navigation and landing aids. It was ready for the first Dash 7 landing in May this year.

One of the airport's most obvious and vital features is the 8,000 square metre terminal, which is covered in a striking blue aluminium and will enable passengers to pass easily through to aircraft parked alongside the 300-metre-long pier.

Waiting passengers will have a clear view of the docks and aircraft movements, while the interior design is deliberately kept simple and classic to enable fast departure – it is claimed that a passenger can be airborne within 15 minutes of arrival at the airport – and yet the terminal is designed to be an extension of the office.

This basic belief – that the passenger should be able to use the airport as easily as he does his own office – dominates the design and philosophy behind the entire concept. The airport will not be for the man or woman who is looking for the cheapest way to fly and is targeted almost exclusively for the business passenger.

But the most important of all is the business centre which, when it is opened in December, will be on the first floor and will be open from 7.30am to 8.30pm.

It seems that everything is now in place. All that is needed now is an influx of passengers.

Harvey Elliott
Air Correspondent

THE HISTORIC COLLECTION

We devote this two-page double-spread to some of the famous and not so famous aircraft that have met both the CAA and the airport's requirements and have graced London City Airport over the 30 years mainly on the 'Fundays' at the weekend on a Saturday afternoon and Sunday morning, when the airport is normally closed.

Above left: *Lady wingwalkers. At one of the open days the Utterly Butterly team gave a display with their Boeing Stearman PT-17.*

Left: *Lufthansa's Junkers Ju 52/3m D-AQUI first flew in 1936.*

Below: *The 2011 'Funday' with some of the aircraft in the line-up. Note at back P-51D WZ-I* Big Beautiful Doll. *More than 15,000 North American Mustangs were built, many serving with the RAF.*

Above: *With a 40m wingspan the largest ever aircraft to land at London City Airport was a military Hercules bringing in the RAF Regiment Band.*

Right: *British Eagle was an early independent competitor to BOAC. Douglas DC6 G-APSA is still around and visited LCY on an Open Day.*

Right: *Two-seater Spitfire trainer at an Open Day.*

Right: *Polly Vacher gained an MBE for the disabled air scholarship work. She also flew this Piper Dakota around the world. Fun Day July 2007.*

1987

Passenger total 15,000.

February: London City Airport was officially named by the Lord Mayor of London Sir David Rowe-Ham. LCY was confirmed as the official designator of the International Air Transport Association (IATA), the trade association of most of the world's international airlines. Not all airlines are members, however, including several low-cost carriers such as easyJet (UK), Ryanair (Ireland), Wizz Air (Hungary) and Southwest Airlines (USA). The International Civil Aviation Organisation (ICAO) code for London City Airport is EGLC. Montreal-based it is a specialised division of the United Nations focussing on standards and safety.

April: Brymon Airways and Eurocity Express were granted route licences by the Civil Aviation Authority (CAA) with Brymon Airways winning a lucrative partnership with Air France for a Paris Charles de Gaulle service, mainly due to Chief Executive Charles Stuart's perfect French and a good relationship with the higher echelons when at British Airways. (Air France was the airline with the longest continuous London City Airport involvement, until March 2017, when they closed the route to Paris Orly.)

31 May: Brymon Airways Dash 7 (G-BRYA) landed and became the first aircraft to operate in and out of London City Airport.

26 October: Brymon Airways and Eurocity Express start commercial flights with Dash 7s. The first inbound was Brymon Airways from Plymouth City Airport and the first outbound Eurocity Express to Paris Charles de Gaulle. Eurocity Express also introduced Brussels National Airport.

5 November: Official opening by Queen Elizabeth, who arrived in her Rolls-Royce, much appreciated by the local residents. Charles Stuart and Eurocity Chairman Michael Bishop (later Lord Glendonbrook) were standing at the bottom of the steps of their respective airline's aircraft waiting to be presented to Queen Elizabeth. When she came to speak to Charles Stuart he invited her to climb the stairs and take a look inside the aircraft. Her Majesty took up the offer and disappeared from sight for a few minutes. Mr Bishop was irked, which was obvious to all involved watching the proceedings.

What was unusual was Queen Elizabeth's departure from dockside London City Airport on the *Royal Nore*, via the King George V lock into the Thames and down to Westminster Pier. It is not known what she said passing the Tower of London but it is rumoured that she was absorbed by the airport and passed on her experience to Prince Philip. His Royal Highness, always an aviation fan, accompanied her on two subsequent visits.

18 December: Flights to Paris Charles de Gaulle were suspended by the CAA because of air traffic conflict safety fears over Kent.

In those early weeks getting to London City Airport was not easy. There was no direct surface access from the City or the A13 and the all-important North Circular Road (A406). Arrivals by train needed to take the grim North London Line railway to Silvertown (later renamed Silvertown for London City Airport) and find their way through a local housing estate.

Taxis were not keen to deliver clients to the airport, because they could have a long wait for a return fare, but the introduction by Mowlem of a free coffee shop seemed to do the trick.

Terry Waite (right) was kidnapped in Beirut. He was to remain captured for 1,763 days before being reunited with his mentor Lord Runcie, Archbishop of Canterbury.

The year that London City Airport opened was also the same year that British Airways was privatised and listed on the London Stock Exchange. Sir John (later Lord) King was Chairman and wasted no time in acquiring British Caledonian Airways. (Dan-Air followed in 1992 and British Midland in 2012.)

British stories of note included the Zeebrugge ferry disaster, the Hungerford Massacre, the Great Storm, Black Monday and the King's Cross fire.

On 6 March the car ferry MS *Herald of Free Enterprise*, which started its journey in Dover, capsized off Zeebrugge harbour in Belgium, killing 193 people. Although the immediate cause of the sinking was found to be negligence by the assistant boatswain, the official inquiry placed more blame on his supervisors and a general culture of poor communication.

In August Michael Robert Ryan shot and killed 16 people at various locations, before committing suicide in the Hungerford massacre – at the time the worst British mass shooting.

The Great Storm of 15–16 October brought hurricane-force winds of up to 120 miles per hour hitting much of southern England, and killing 22 people. Just three days later Black Monday saw stock market levels fall sharply – the crash began in Far Eastern markets the morning of 19 October, but accelerated once the London Stock Exchange opened. London had closed early on the previous Friday due to the storm. By 09:30 the London FTSE100 had fallen over 136 points.

The King's Cross fire of 18 November on the London Underground killed 31 people and injured a further 100. The inquiry determined that the fire had started due to a lit match being dropped onto the wooden escalator. As a result of the inquiry wooden escalators were eventually replaced with metal ones.

Terry Waite, the special envoy of the Archbishop of Canterbury in Lebanon, was kidnapped in Beirut; Margaret Thatcher was re-elected as Prime Minister; the Docklands Light Railway (DLR), the first driverless passenger train service in the United Kingdom was formally opened by Queen Elizabeth and on 8 November, 12 people were killed by a Provisional Irish Republican Army bomb at a Remembrance Day service at Enniskillen.

In news around the world, President Reagan told the American people that he took full responsibility for the arms-for-hostages crisis, otherwise known as the Iran Contra Affair – although to this day Reagan's role in the transactions is not definitively known. It was also the year that 18-year-old West German pilot Mathias Rust evaded Soviet air defences and landed a private plane on Red Square in Moscow. In entertainment *The Simpsons* cartoon first appeared as a series of shorts on *The Tracey Ullman Show* and Michael Jackson released his *Bad* album.

In sport Nelson Piquet of Brazil won the F1 World Championship, Pat Cash won Wimbledon and Everton were First Division champions. The first Rugby World Cup was co-hosted by New Zealand and Australia with New Zealand eventually winning the cup.

Famous people that died included Andy Warhol, artist; Fred Astaire, dancer; Rita Hayworth, actress; Danny Kaye, actor; Dean Martin, actor; Rudolf Hess, Nazi Deputy Führer and Eamon Andrews, radio and television presenter best known for *This Is Your Life*.

1988

Passenger total 133,000.

20 January: Brymon Airways resumed its six times daily service to Paris Charles de Gaulle, in conjunction with Air France, with among the passengers BBC presenter Gloria Hunniford who, on the spur of the moment, thought it would be a good piece. Catching the 07:00 outbound, she was back at Broadcasting House for her 14:00 radio show.

The airport launched a 35-minute Riverbus service to and from Embankment. Airport passengers disembarked at the Charrington Pier on the River Thames with a short coach connection to the terminal. It was popular with passengers but less so with Mowlem, who lost money. Radio connection confirmed passengers and flights. Aircraft were known to wait.

Eurocity Express changed its name to London City Airways and in October concluded a deal to codeshare with the then Belgian national airline Sabena on a new route to Brussels National Airport.

19 June: Bill Lindsell was appointed London City Airport Director.

24 July: Successful demonstration flight by a Loganair BAe 146.

A poll noted 83% of local residents were in favour of the BAe 146 jet being allowed to fly from London City Airport.

At the original Heron Quays Docklands Light Railway (DLR) station platform there was a small plaque unveiling ceremony to commemorate the trial Dash 7 landings there in 1982 and 1983.

Construction started at Canary Wharf.

Private jets began to use the airport.

Above: *Scottish airline Loganair brought in a BAe 146 to demonstrate to the public how quiet a jet could be.*

Below: *This was the aircraft that did not make LCY. An artist impression of the BAe 146 in Brymon Airways colours.*

George H. Bush becomes US President.

Terrorist attacks were major news in the UK.

During the funeral in Northern Ireland on 16 March of three Irish Republican Army (IRA) members killed in Gibraltar, loyalist paramilitary Michael Stone murdered three mourners and left 70 wounded. Stone was eventually overpowered and arrested by members of the Royal Ulster Constabulary.

On the morning of 12 December, a crowded passenger train crashed into the rear of another train that had stopped at a signal, just south of Clapham Junction railway station in London, and subsequently sideswiped an empty train travelling in the opposite direction. A total of 35 people were killed in the collision, while 484 were injured. The subsequent investigation found that the collision was the result of a signal failure caused by a wiring fault. British Rail was fined £250,000 for violations of health and safety law in connection with the incident.

On 21 December all 243 passengers and 16 crew were killed on Pam Am Flight 103, a transatlantic flight from Frankfurt to Detroit via London and New York – the attack later became known as the Lockerbie bombing. Large sections of the aircraft crashed onto residential areas of Lockerbie, Scotland, killing 11 more people on the ground. A Libyan intelligence officer was jailed for life in connection with the bombings – the only person ever to be convicted. However, in 2003 Libyan leader Muammar Gaddafi accepted responsibility for the Lockerbie bombing and paid compensation to the families of the victims – although he maintained that he had never given the order for the attack.

In British politics the Liberal Democrat Party was formed, a merger between the Liberals and the Social Democrats, after disappointing results in the 1987 elections. Paddy Ashdown was elected its leader. It was the same year that the £1 note ceased to be legal tender.

George H. W. Bush became the first sitting Vice-President of the United States in 152 years to be elected as President in 1988. The other major story in the USA was the trial of Lieutenant Colonel Oliver North and Vice-Admiral John Poindexter for their part in the arms for cash scandal, otherwise known as the Iran-Contra affair.

Other international events included: al-Qaeda being formed by Osama bin Laden; the end of the Iran-Iraq War; François Mitterrand being re-elected Prime Minister of France and Benazzir Bhutto to the same position in Pakistan. A concert was held at Wembley Stadium to mark Nelson Mandela's 70th birthday, which had an estimated global audience of 600 million.

Sport news was dominated by the Summer Olympics in Seoul, South Korea. Team GB won five golds (including golds for Steve Redgrave in rowing, Adrian Moorhouse in swimming) ten silver and nine bronze. Canadian Ben Johnson won the 100-metre final with a new world record, but was later disqualified after he tested positive for the illegal drug, stanozolol.

Other major sporting events included the Winter Olympics in Calgary, Canada; the UEFA football cup was won by West German team Bayer Leverkusen (English teams were barred following the 1985 Heysel disaster); and the Rugby World Cup won by its hosts, Australia.

Famous people who died include Roy Orbison, singer; Roy Kinnear, actor and comedian (and father of actor Rory Kinnear), and Kenneth Williams, comedy actor.

1989

Passenger total 216,000.

Passenger increase of 62% on the previous year.
Number of flights 10,764, up 30%.

Brymon Airways Chief Executive, Charles Stuart, called for a DLR link to the airport.

In the spring, Flexair (later to become VLM) introduced a service to Rotterdam with a Dornier 228 turboprop. It had started as a weekly charter flight bringing in labour to work on the rebuilding of Liverpool Street station. It was noisy and cramped but did the job and with the word getting around became a daily service.

Aberdeen-based Business Air Centre arrived with an 18-seat DHC Twin Otter utility aircraft available for charter. (Bought later by British Midland Airways).

Brymon Airways took delivery of a 35-seat DHC Dash 8 twin turboprop. (This would later be developed into the 78-seat Bombardier Q400).

October: London City Airport submitted a Planning Application to extend the runway, allowing the airport to serve more distant destinations with a broader range of aircraft.

A London Underground connection for the airport was highlighted at Highbury & Islington Station. This was part of the North London Line which stopped at the renamed Silvertown for London City Airport station on its way to North Woolwich. The airport terminal, closed on a Saturday evening, hosted a concert by the Docklands Sinfonietta. The performance was restricted to 200, tickets costing £75 each. Profits went to Barnardo's children's charity.

London City Airport won a competition for 'Loo of the Year'.

The Eastern Access road was opened in October linking the A13 to North Woolwich and the airport. (This would later join the Royal Albert Dock Spine Road and connect to the new Connaught Crossing Bridge to the west of the airport.)

Brymon Airways was joint runner-up with British Airways in the UK Domestic Airlines category at the *Executive Travel* awards held at London's Grosvenor House Hotel. In accepting the award Charles Stuart called for London City Airport to be replicated on land between Heathrow and the M4 as a quick way of increasing provincial slots at Heathrow (then the world's busiest international airport).

London City Airport is unique in that it is closed from lunchtime Saturday until lunchtime Sunday offering an opportunity for social events in the terminal. An orchestral concert was held in the early days, and seen here, a party for the locals.

Steffi Graf takes Wimbledon for the second time – She eventually gained seven victories.

In Britain two disasters, both health and safety related, were the focus of British media attention. On 15 April the crush of supporters at the Hillsborough Stadium, the home of Sheffield Wednesday, during an FA Cup semi-final match between Liverpool and Nottingham Forest left 96 Liverpool Football Club supporters dead. And on 20 August, 51 people died when the *Marchioness* pleasure boat collided with a barge on the River Thames. Long and complex investigations occurred after both disasters and the conclusions led to improvements in safety both at football grounds and on the river.

Other British news included the release on 19 October of the 'Guildford Four', who had been convicted of bombings carried out by the Provisional Irish Republican Army.

It was a historic year internationally as the 'Revolutions' of the old Eastern Bloc saw the beginning of the end of the Cold War and the setting up of democratic states in previously communist countries. Major protests took place in East Germany (Leipzig – 300,000 people) and Czechoslovakia (Letná Square – 800,000 people).

Against a backdrop of an unstable economy and limited political freedom over one million people protested in Tiananmen Square, Beijing, China. The protests were forcibly suppressed after the government declared martial law in what became widely known as the Tiananmen Square Massacre.

The year also saw changes in the way that Albania, Bulgaria, Hungary, Poland, Romania and Yugoslavia were politically run. On 23 December visa-free travelling was finally allowed between East and West Germany after several gaps were made in the Berlin Wall by protesters.

In other steps for democracy, the President of South Africa P. W. Botha (who had just been elected) met the imprisoned Nelson Mandela face-to-face; Brazil held its first presidential elections in 29 years (won by Fernando Collor de Mello of the now-defunct National Reconstruction Party) and France celebrated the 200th anniversary of the French Revolution.

On 8 January – the Kegworth air disaster: a British Midland Boeing 737 crashed onto the M1 motorway on the approach to East Midlands Airport, killing 44 people. On 8 September – a Partnair Convair 580 disintegrated over the North Sea. Although the cause was disputed, the owners claimed that a USAF F-16 Fighting Falcon had flown past at supersonic speed causing shock waves. The aircraft's service records were poor. Also in 1989, Surinam Airways Flight 764 crashed in Paramaribo, Surinam, killing 176 people and United Airlines Douglas DC-10 which made a (semi) controlled crash landing at Sioux City Airport after the tail-mounted engine had failed, killing 112 people; 184 on board survived. (In some ways the flying was even more remarkable than the miracle on the Hudson River, New York, in 2016.)

Chelsea beat Portsmouth in the FA Cup, Steffi Graf and Boris Becker of West Germany won their respective singles titles at Wimbledon. England held Sweden to a 0–0 draw in Sweden, qualifying for the 1990 FIFA World Cup.

It was the year of the death of three significant political figures: Hirohito, Emperor of Japan; Ayatollah Ruhollah Khomeini, Supreme Leader of Iran; and Nicolae Ceausescu, Romanian dictator, together with his wife Elena, who were both executed. Other notables who died were Irving Berlin, composer of *White Christmas* who passed away at the age of 101; Bette Davis, actress; Daphne du Maurier, author; Lord (Laurence) Olivier, actor and director, and Samuel Beckett, Irish writer and Nobel Prize laureate.

1990

Passenger total 230,000.

Passenger increase of 6% on the previous year.
Number of flights 13,135, up 22%.

Airport Director Bill Lindsell retired and was succeeded by William (Bill) Charnock.

July: A Public Inquiry opened into jet services to operate concurrently with the turboprops already licensed. It was to last, with summer and Christmas breaks, until January 1991.

London City Airways was absorbed into British Midland Airways and left the airport.

Published fares for the Riverbus service from London City Airport were £4.80 to both London Bridge City on the south side of the Thames and Swann Lane on the north bank, and £6.00 from Embankment to Charing Cross. At this time the service was up to three per hour and 26% of Brymon Airways' passengers used it.

There were further awards for Brymon Airways at the *Air Transport World* 'Commuter Airline of the Year'. The carrier, with its Air France partnership, made much of its early 07:00 departure to Paris Charles de Gaulle Airport complete with Champagne breakfast. Brymon Airways' Charles Stuart, and a small press party, were offered by Air France the 10:00 Concorde departure from Paris to New York to collect the trophy. Sadly Paris fogged in and they (just) made the 10:00 British Airways' Heathrow departure, in those days from Terminal 4.

Brymon Airways added Lille, Nantes and Strasbourg at the request of Air France.

Above: *Before trains. An early visitor was Michael Portillo (right), with his Secretary of State for Transport hat on, seen here with Robert Hardless, then with Brymon Airways.*

Left: *The original check-in area with natural lighting through the transparent roof. Seen left is John Horne, later to be Airport Director, and far right Nicholas Hopkins, Mowlem PRO.*

Margaret Thatcher resigns after 11 years as Prime Minister.

In Britain 200,000 people protested against the Poll Tax on 31 March, a council tax based on the number of people living in a property rather than the property's value. The protest led to rioting and the unpopular policy was a significant factor in the Conservative Prime Minister Margaret Thatcher's resignation on 22 November. She was succeeded by John Major.

Other British news included the riot at Strangeways prison, Manchester, in April which lasted over three weeks – the longest riot in British history. One prisoner died, 147 prison officers and 47 prisoners were injured and the riot caused over £50 million in damages. On 30 July the Irish Republican Army blew up Member of Parliament Ian Gow with a car bomb outside his home – the reason they gave was because he was a 'close personal associate' of the then Prime Minister Margaret Thatcher. Also in 1990, the first women were ordained as Anglican priests.

Following the mostly peaceful revolutions in 1989, over 25 countries, mostly from the old Soviet Bloc, had democratic elections for the first time in recent history. These took place in Czechoslovakia, East Germany, Hungary, Russian SFSR, Serbia and Ukraine. East and West Germany merged and with it the destruction of the Berlin Wall.

Mikhail Gorbachev, the President of the Soviet Union, was honoured for his efforts to bring peace to the region by winning the Nobel Peace Prize and Western leaders met to officially mark the end of the Cold War. Free elections were also held in Brazil and Chile.

On 6 March a Lockheed SR-71, known as the Blackbird, crossed North America in 1 hour 7 minutes 54 seconds at an average speed of 2,242 miles per hour, an air speed record, which as of July 2017 still holds.

In other international news the United States invaded Panama on 3 January. Nelson Mandela was freed after 27 years behind bars on 11 February; the Hubble Space Telescope (HST) was launched into low earth orbit on 24 April; the invasion of Kuwait by Iraq, on 2 August (which eventually led to the Gulf War); and on

1 November Mary Robinson became the first female President of Ireland.

In sport Buster Douglas defeated Mike Tyson by a knockout in round ten to win the world heavyweight title, in what many consider boxing's biggest upset ever; West Germany won the FIFA World Cup in Rome in its final tournament before national reunification, defeating defending champion Argentina 1–0 in the final and Ayrton Senna was world motor racing champion.

The Hollywood stars Greta Garbo, Ava Gardner and Sammy Davies Jnr all died along with Roald Dahl, the famous children's author.

1991

Passenger total 172,000.

Passenger numbers were down by 25% on the previous year.
Number of flights 9,631, down 27%.

Secretary of State for the Environment Michael Heseltine approved London City Airport's expansion plans.

Business Air Centre commenced a short-lived service to Frankfurt using a BAe 146. It was the end of their interest in the airport.

Canary Wharf, at the time Europe's tallest building, was completed.

American Airlines arrived at Heathrow Airport buying the TWA slots and Delta took over much of Pan Am. US inbound passengers making for Europe were not even made aware of the existence of London City Airport.

As a result of the Gulf War and the loss of London City Airways, passenger numbers fell dramatically. Brymon Airways struggled on with joint Air France services to Paris Charles de Gaulle, Lille and Strasbourg.

The BAe J41 Jetstream turboprop made its first flight but the 29-seater was really too small for London City Airport and had no impact. The much larger BAe 146 jet, capable of carrying 112 passengers, was approved for London City Airport; and Brymon Airways organised a high-profile press briefing to announce its interest.

British Air Ferries (later to become British World Airlines) said it was coming into London City Airport, but it never happened.

Above: *The original first floor landside brasserie.*

Below: *The river boat service from Charing Cross proved very popular in spite of a short coach ride at the airport end.*

Robert Maxwell fell off his yacht *Lady Ghislaine* – his body was later recovered.

The Provisional Irish Republican Army (IRA) were the focus of several major news stories.

On 7 February a bomb struck Downing Street whilst a cabinet meeting was taking place. Due to bomb-proof windows none of the cabinet were hurt, though four other people received minor injuries. Eleven days later on the 18 February the group attacked Paddington and Victoria stations, killing one person and injuring 38.

The Provisional IRA were in the news for a different reason on the 14 March when the 'Birmingham Six' were released after being erroneously imprisoned for 16 years for the 'Birmingham pub bombings', in which 21 people died. Their convictions were declared unjust and unsatisfactory and were quashed by the Court of Appeal. The six were awarded compensation ranging from £840,000 to £1.2 million.

In other British news, on 5 November Robert Maxwell, the media proprietor and former MP, made his last contact with the crew of the *Lady Ghislaine*, his yacht which was cruising off the Canary Islands. He was found to be missing later in the morning and his body was subsequently recovered from the Atlantic Ocean. Suicide was ruled out and the inquest found that his death was caused by a heart attack combined with accidental drowning. He was presumed to have fallen overboard from the vessel.

In international news, the initial conflict to expel Iraqi troops from Kuwait began with an aerial and naval bombardment on 17 January that continued for five weeks. It was followed by a ground assault on 24 February and was a decisive victory for the coalition forces, who liberated Kuwait and declared a ceasefire 100 hours after the ground campaign started. Aerial and ground combat was confined to Iraq, Kuwait and areas on Saudi Arabia's border.

Another major story was the dissolution of the Soviet Union on 26 December. This created the Commonwealth of Independent States (CIS). On the previous day, Soviet President Mikhail Gorbachev resigned, declared his office extinct, and handed over its powers – including control of the Soviet nuclear missile launching codes – to Russian President Boris Yeltsin.

Former Prime Minister of India, Rajiv Gandhi, was killed by a suicide bomber at a public meeting on 22 May; Bank of Credit and Commerce International became the focus of a massive regulatory battle in 1991, and, on 5 July of that year, customs and bank regulators in seven countries raided and locked down records of its branch offices. In July the boxer Mike Tyson was arrested and charged with the rape of Miss Black America contestant Desiree Washington. On 6 August the first website, invented by Tim Berners-Lee, went online. American journalist Terry Anderson was released after seven years of captivity in Beirut on 4 December.

In sport Mike Powell broke Bob Beamon's 23-year-old long jump world record with a mark of 29 feet 4½ inches which stands to this day; Los Angeles Lakers point guard Magic Johnson announced that he had HIV, effectively ending his NBA career, and Manchester United won the European Cup Winners' Cup with a 2–1 win over FC Barcelona in Rotterdam.

Notable deaths included Freddie Mercury, lead singer of Queen; Miles Davies, the jazz musician as well as Robert Maxwell, publisher.

1992

Passenger total 186,000.

Passenger numbers were down by 25% on the previous year.
Number of flights 9,631, down 27%.

5 March: Diana, Princess of Wales visited London City Airport to open the newly-extended runway.

March: BAe 146 jet flights began with the first Crossair scheduled operation to Zurich. Moritz Suter, Managing Director of the Swiss airline, was very much a fan of London City Airport and welcomed Sir Colin Marshall, Chief Executive of British Airways, on an early service.

Away from the airport, but a more serious casualty, was the collapse of Olympia & York Canary Wharf Ltd in May. The first buildings were completed in 1991, including One Canada Square, which became the UK's tallest building at that date and eventually a symbol of the regeneration of Docklands. By the time it opened, the London commercial property market had collapsed.

June: Bromma, the Stockholm city centre airport, became another London City Airport destination, two flights daily with a Malmö Aviation BAe 146, flying as Cityair Scandinavia. The airline's UK Director Robert Hardless came out strongly in favour of the proposed Jubilee Line extension to Canary Wharf.

October: Mowlem announced its intention to sell part of its stake in London City Airport.

German airline Conti-Flug introduced twice daily BAe 146 services to Berlin Tempelhof. (Later in the decade the famous city centre airport was to close to make way for Berlin Brandenburg, which at the time of writing is still not open.)

Rotterdam starts with Flexair and a Dornier 228.

Flight numbers continued to decline but the actual throughput of passengers rose with the arrival of more BAe 146 aircraft.

Princess Diana officially opened the extended runway and then departed in a No 32 (Royal) Squadron BAe 146.

Betty Boothroyd became the first woman elected Speaker of the House of Commons.

Queen Elizabeth described 1992 as her *annus horribilis*. It was the year when two of her children, Prince Charles and Prince Andrew, separated from their wives and, another, Princess Anne, divorced. In addition to this there was a major fire at one of her beloved homes – Windsor Castle – with repairs costing £36.5 million.

In politics, the Conservative Party, led by John Major, narrowly won the General Election on 9 April beating Neil Kinnock's Labour Party. On 27 April Betty Boothroyd became the first woman elected Speaker of the House of Commons.

Other British stories included the *Freddie Mercury Tribute Concert* for AIDS research on 20 April, which was held at Wembley Stadium. On 25 October 150,000 miners marched in London to protest government plans to close more than half of Britain's coal mines, but the decision was final. On 3 December the first SMS message was sent over the Vodafone GSM network in the United Kingdom.

Europe also featured strongly in the news. On 7 February the Maastricht Treaty was signed, creating the European Union and on 16 September or 'Black Wednesday', sterling was forced out of the European Exchange Rate Mechanism because the Bank of England was unable to keep it above the agreed limit.

Racism hit American headlines on 3 March in Los Angeles when a passer-by videotaped four officers surrounding Rodney King, a black taxi driver, after a high-speed chase – several of them striking him repeatedly whilst other officers stood by. The video was handed into a local news station and shown around the world and raised concern about the police treatment of minorities in the United States. All four were acquitted. The acquittals are generally considered to have triggered the 1992 Los Angeles riots in which 55 people were killed and 2,000 injured.

Beginning on 9 December about 25,000 United States forces were sent to Mogadishu, Somalia as part of an effort to restore peace to the region.

Other news stories included the opening of Euro Disney in Paris on 12 April and the end of satirical British magazine *Punch*. It published its final issue after 150 years due to falling sales and subscriptions.

In sport the Barcelona Summer Olympic Games were held. South Africa was allowed to compete for the first time since 1960 and the Baltic nations of Estonia, Latvia and Lithuania contested the games, 1936 being their last appearance. Great Britain won five gold medals with Linford Christie (100 metres), Sally Gunnell (women's 400 metres hurdles), Chris Boardman (cycling), the men's coxless pairs in rowing with Matthew Pinsent and Steve Redgrave and the Searle brothers Greg and Johnny, coxed by Garry Herber.

Famous people who died included Isaac Asimov, author; Benny Hill comedian; Menachem Begin, Prime Minister of Israel and recipient of the Nobel Peace Prize; and Marlene Dietrich, actress.

1993

Passenger total 245,000.

Passenger increase of 30% on the previous year.
Number of flights 11,663, up 14%.

March: Brymon Airways left London City Airport following a management sale giving 100% ownership to British Airways. Its value was up to five pairs of slots it held at Heathrow.

The Limehouse Link and other Docklands highways opened for traffic.

End of the Riverbus service. The problem was that it did not reach the airport, the King George V Dock only accessible via a lock. (For the 2012 Olympic Games two cruise ships moored opposite the airport to serve as floating hotels.)

Charles Stuart, the much respected Chief Executive of Brymon Airways when the airport opened, passed away suddenly (aged 64). At one time with British Rail, Stuart had instigated the British Airways shuttle and was an elegant spokesman for the airport during its gestation. His contacts at British Airways gained the airport support by the national carrier.

April: Conti-Flug extended its Berlin service to Venice.

A three times per hour bus service was introduced between the airport, Canary Wharf and Liverpool Street station.

October: Canary Wharf emerged from administration.

Also in October a new airline VLM arrived at the airport with a service to Antwerp. (Taken over by Air France in 2007 it was part of CityJet until 2014.)

November: Conti-Flug announced that it would start services to Hamburg, Riga and Vilnius. It never happened, the airline folding during the Farnborough Air Show 1994.

Early days – then a choice of stations.

Nelson Mandela and F. W. de Klerk jointly won the Nobel Peace Prize.

British news was dominated by the murders of Stephen Lawrence and Jamie Bulger.

On 12 February Jamie Bulger, a two-year-old boy from Kirkby, Merseyside, was murdered after two ten-year-old boys, Robert Thompson and Jon Venables, abducted him from a shopping centre in Bootle. They became the youngest convicted murderers in modern English history.

On 22 April Stephen Lawrence, a black man, was murdered in a racially motivated attack in Plumsted, South London. Five suspects were arrested but not convicted. It was one of the highest profile racial killings in United Kingdom history and its fallout included profound cultural changes to attitudes on racism and the police. (After reviewing the case it was found that the Metropolitan Police Service was institutionally racist. Almost 20 years later two juveniles were found guilty of Lawrence's murder.)

In other British news, British Airways' Lord King admitted liability and apologised 'unreservedly' for a 'dirty tricks' campaign against Virgin Atlantic. On 24 April the Irish Republican Army detonated a truck in Bishopsgate, a major thoroughfare in London's financial district, killing one person, injuring 44, and causing £350 million in damages.

Relations between Iraq and the United States deteriorated in 1993. The United States accused Saddam Hussein, the President of Iraq, of moving missiles into southern Iraq. Allied planes and ships destroyed the missile sites, as well as a nuclear facility outside Baghdad. The United States learned of a plot to assassinate the former US President, George Bush, and in response, US ships attacked Iraqi intelligence headquarters in Baghdad.

Notable events included a terrorist attack on the World Trade Centre, New York – a truck bomb detonated below the North Tower, killing six people and injuring over a thousand more; the Oslo Accord was signed between the Palestinian Liberation Organisation (PLO) leader Yasser Arafat and Israeli Prime Minister Yitzhak Rabin.

Nelson Mandela and F.W. de Klerk jointly won the Nobel Peace Prize; the Waco Siege in Texas, which started on 28 February, saw 76 people die after a 51-day stand-off between American forces and Branch Davidians who were suspected of weapon violations; the North American Free Trade Agreement (NAFTA) was signed on 8 December between the United States, Canada and Mexico. The film *Jurassic Park* was the big hit – it topped the box office charts but did poorly in the Oscars – *Schindler's List*, the holocaust epic, was also released.

In sport the 1993 FA Cup final between Arsenal and Sheffield Wednesday at Wembley finished 1–1 with the Gunners winning the replay 2–1 after extra-time. They became the first English side to achieve a domestic cup double, having also won the 1993 Football League Cup final. The English Premier League was created the previous year, with Manchester United becoming the first winners.

Famous people who died in 1993 included Audrey Hepburn, actress; Ferruccio Lamborghini, founder of the car company; Bobby Moore, footballer; and William Golding, author.

1994

Passenger total 480,000.

Passenger increase of 96% on the previous year.
Number of flights 16,845, up 48%.

The airport was now into a steady period of growth.

Passenger numbers nearly doubled over the previous year with airlines trying new routes and the word getting around that the airport had a lot to offer. Crossair introduced Geneva.

11 January: Richard Branson turned up at the airport to welcome the inaugural Virgin CityJet flight from Dublin. On board was CityJet CEO Pat Byrne.

CityJet arrived from Dublin with a BAe 146, initially in partnership with Virgin Atlantic Airways. This relationship quickly floundered. (CityJet has been a stalwart of the airport ever since and is now (2017) back with the original owners and under the chairmanship of Pat Byrne, the founding Chief Executive.)

5 July: The Sunday Trading Act comes into full effect, permitting retailers to trade on Sundays. The planning restrictions for the airport do not allow landings or take-offs between the hours of 06:30 and 12:30 on a Saturday and 12:30 and 22:00 on a Sunday unless an emergency. (This remains in force, although for practical reasons the doors of the terminal actually open to the public at 11:00 on Sundays.)

14 November: The start of a new rail service – Eurostar – linking London's Waterloo station with Brussels (and Paris) in only just over two hours, made the air service to Brussels unviable. (The rail journey is now under two hours but from St Pancras. Paris flights continued until 2017.) London City Airport is now the only UK departure point for Paris Orly, which serves the Left Bank and is some way from Gare du Nord the terminal from London.

Virgin had a short-lived relationship with CityJet who repainted a BAe 146.

The Channel Tunnel opened – French President François Mitterrand and the Queen.

In February British police began excavations at 25 Cromwell Street, Gloucester, the home of Fred and Rosemary West. The Wests were accused of multiple murders and it was found that sexual assault, torture, as well as dismembering of bodies had taken place. Remains of some of the bodies were found in their cellar and garden, leading the media to call their home the 'House of Horrors'. Fred West was later found guilty of at least 12 murders and Rose 10, although the actual figures are suspected to be much higher.

In other British news, on 26 January a man fired two blank shots at Prince Charles in Sydney, Australia; on 13 June the Channel Tunnel opened and with it the introduction of train travel between London and both Brussels and Paris; the Sunday Trading Act 1994 came into full effect on 5 July , permitting retailers to trade on Sundays; Tony Blair gained the Labour Party leadership after an election and the Camelot Group consortium won the contract to run the United Kingdom's first National Lottery with the initial draw taking place on 19 November.

It was also the year that the Irish and British Governments announced the end of a 15-year broadcasting ban on the Provisional Irish Republican Army and its political arm Sinn Fein meaning that the real voices of Jeremy Adams and his comrades could be heard by audiences for the first time.

In international news O. J. Simpson, the American football player, was arrested for the murders of his ex-wife and her friend on 13 June. He was later acquitted but in 1997 was convicted of numerous felonies, including armed robbery and kidnapping. The case has been described as the most publicized criminal trial in American history.

In other international news, on 27 April Nelson Mandela was inaugurated as South Africa's first black President; on 25 July Israel and Jordan signed the Washington Declaration peace treaty which settled relations between the two countries, adjusted land and water disputes, and provided for broad cooperation in tourism and trade; and on 11 December Russian President Boris Yeltsin ordered troops into Chechnya.

Two major world sporting events took place – the Winter Olympics in Lillehammer and the FIFA World Cup hosted by the United States. In the Olympics, Jayne Torvill and Christopher Dean won a controversial bronze medal in ice skating for Team GB. In the World Cup, Brazil beat Italy by 3–2 in penalties. England failed to qualify for the competition. It was also the year that Manchester United achieved a League and Cup double.

There were many notable deaths including, Richard Nixon, President of the United States; John Smith, leader of the Labour Party; Sir Matt Busby, Manchester United football manager; Jacqueline Kennedy Onassis, First Lady of the United States and Ayrton Senna, F1 racing driver, killed in an accident during the San Marino Grand Prix in Imola, Italy.

1995

Passenger total 555,946.

Passenger increase of 15% on the previous year.
Number of flights 18,562, up 16%.

March: Jon Horne promoted to Airport Director on a temporary basis, Bill Charnock departing.

The airport introduced the first ticketless air travel in the UK and Air Jet was launched on the Paris Charles de Gaulle route with a prepaid 'jet card' system which also eliminated multi-folio paper tickets. The airline did not last long.

Carriers came and went and 12 points were served. These included City Air Bus to Humberside Airport (south of Hull) with four flights. It flew for just a few weeks with the company going into liquidation. Air Engiadina was to become another short-lived airline to Bern, but the route remains to this day operated over the years by several different carriers.

Interot arrived with a Dash 8 from Augsburg. Starting off as a company aircraft owner using two Beech aircraft in support of its printing paper manufacture, Interot later became Augsburg Airways operating all four versions of the Dash 8 and Embraers as 'Team Lufthansa', until Lufthansa pulled the plug in 2013.

Sir Philip Beck retired as Chairman of John Mowlem & Co Plc, the developer of London City Airport, and just a few weeks later the airport was sold to Irish businessman Dermot Desmond for a reputed £23.5 million.

Left: *At one time VLM operated up to 20 Fokker 50s.*

Below left: *Interot was predecessor to Augusburg Airways.*

Fred Perry (right) died – he won Wimbledon three times 1934–1936 (seen here with Bunny Austin).

This was the year the United Kingdom's oldest investment banking firm – Barings Bank – collapsed after securities broker Nick Leeson lost $1.4 billion by speculating on the Tokyo Stock Exchange. He was arrested in Frankfurt and extradited to Singapore and later sentenced to six and a half years in prison.

Other news included John Major resignation as leader of the Conservative Party on 22 June in order to trigger a leadership battle so that he could face the critics of his Party. He was re-elected on 4 July beating the only other candidate, former Secretary of State for Wales, John Redwood. On 20 November Princess Diana gave a revealing television interview on BBC One's *Panorama* show where she candidly discussed her adultery, depression and bulimia.

1995 was the first year that British soldiers were not patrolling the streets in Belfast since 1969.

In Europe, Austria, Finland and Sweden joined the European Union and Jacques Chirac was elected President of France. The Schengen Agreement, which invoked a European-wide passport free area, came into effect between all countries in the European Union excluding the United Kingdom and Ireland.

The biggest news story of the year in the United States was the Oklahoma City bombing. On 19 April Timothy McVeigh murdered 168 people, including 8 federal marshals and 19 children; 680 people were also wounded. McVeigh was motivated by the Federal Government's handling of the Waco siege and the bombing coincided with the second anniversary of the deadly fire that ended the siege. Found guilty of 11 Federal offences McVeigh was later executed by lethal injection. Terry Nichols and Michael Fortier were also convicted as conspirators in the plot.

On the wider international stage, the World Trade Organization (WTO) was established on 1 January to replace the General Agreement on Tariffs and Trade (GATT).

In July, the worst crime on European soil since World War II took place in and around the Bosnian town of Srebrenica. It was perpetrated by units of the Bosnian Serb Army of Republika Srpska (VRS) under the command of General Ratko Mladić, together with the Scorpions, a paramilitary unit, participating in the massacre of more than 8,000 Bosniak men and boys together with the forcible transfer and abuse of between 25,000 and 30,000 Bosniak women, children and elderly. The besieged enclave of Srebrenica had been declared a 'safe area' under United Nations Protection Force. However UNPROFOR's 370 Dutchbat soldiers failed to prevent the town's capture by the VRS. The United Nations tribunal on human rights charged up to 60 Bosnian Serb commanders with genocide and crimes against humanity.

In football the UEFA Champions League was won by AFC Ajax when they beat AC Milan 1–0 at the Ernst Happel Stadium in Vienna. It will also be remembered as the year that Eric Catona, of Manchester United, infamously 'Kung Fu' attacked a football fan at Crystal Palace. Catona received an eight month ban from playing football competitively. In rugby, South Africa, the hosts of the World Cup won the competition when they beat New Zealand 15–12. In boxing Frank Bruno won the WBC world heavyweight championship after defeating Oliver McCall at a packed Wembley Stadium.

Famous people that died included Fred Perry, tennis champion; Kenny Everett, comedian; Lord (Harold) Wilson and Lord Hume (Alex Douglas-Hume), Prime Ministers of the United Kingdom; Eva Gabor, actress; and Paul Eddington, actor.

1996

Passenger total 726,000.

Passenger increase of 41% on the previous year.
Number of flights 27,059, up 31%.

Among the visiting aircraft during the year was a Royal Air Force Hercules transport carrying the Band of the RAF Regiment which played on the apron. A Spitfire was another new type to land.

Appointment of new London City Airport Chairman, Ray MacSharry.

Richard Gooding, previously Managing Director of Luton Airport, was appointed Managing Director.

World Airlines came on the Amsterdam route and quickly went bust.

A new baggage screening system, said to be as good as anywhere in the world, was installed at a cost of over £1 million.

Also good news was the growth in passenger numbers to 4,000 a day.

The two routes to Paris were not that far apart in terms of numbers, Charles de Gaulle at 43,000 and Orly 34,000. Air France decided that the south Paris airport made more sense for business travellers than CDG and closed what was London City Airport's original international route. In comparison 150,000 used Dublin.

By this time, the Netherlands had also begun to take an interest in the airport, Rotterdam with 75,000 and the newly reconstituted Amsterdam CityJet service 48,000. Frankfurt grew by 10% to 47,000. New were Edinburgh and Eindhoven.

March: Fokker Aircraft based at Amsterdam Schiphol Airport finally went bankrupt and ceased manufacturing the F-50 (turboprop) and F-70 and F-100 (jet turbine). This followed the withdrawal of DASA (Daimler-Benz) from the partnership. This had no immediate effect on Amsterdam as one of Europe's largest scheduled airports but it meant an uncertain future for the Fokker operators. Thanks, however, to subsidiary Fokker companies not affected by the upheaval, more than 20 years on Fokker passenger aircraft are still in airline service in 2017.

Richard Gooding (left) seen here with Reg Ward and TfL's Ian Brown at a 2007 ceremony to unveil a plaque for Harry Gee's first landing at Heron Quays.

Germany won the European Championship with England's Alan Shearer the top scorer.

The year was marked with Irish Republican Army terrorist activity. The IRA ended their ceasefire on 9 February when a bomb near South Quay station in the Canary Wharf, London, exploded. Two people were killed and £150 million of damage caused. A few weeks later on 18 February a further IRA bomb killed one person and injured another in the West End of London. On 7 June an IRA gang killed Detective Garda Jerry McCabe during a botched armed robbery in Adare, County Limerick. In Manchester on 15 June a truck bomb detonated in the city centre causing over 200 injuries but no fatalities. It was the biggest bomb detonated in Great Britain since World War II causing damage estimated at £700 million. Finally on 13 July a bomb exploded outside a hotel in Enniskillen, Northern Ireland, disrupting a wedding reception and injuring 17 people.

In a deadly attack of a different nature, gunman Thomas Hamilton killed 16 children and one teacher on 13 March at Dunblane Primary School near Stirling, Scotland, before killing himself. The attack, which became known as the Dunblane School Massacre, was the deadliest mass shooting in the United Kingdom's history. Public debate about the killings centred on gun control laws, including public petitions calling for a ban on private ownership of handguns. In response to this debate, two new firearms acts were passed, which greatly restricted private ownership of firearms in Great Britain.

On 20 March the UK Government announced that Bovine spongiform encephalopathy, also known as BSE or mad cow disease, had likely been transmitted to humans. This led to the European Union banning exports of British beef, a ban which lasted ten years. Estimates suggested that from 1986–1998 more than 180,000 cattle were infected and 4.4 million were slaughtered during the eradication programme.

The Scott Report was published, in effect a judicial inquiry investigating arms sales to Iraq. The examination, conducted by Sir Richard Scott, then a Lord Justice of Appeal, was partially redacted and never published in full.

In the United States the First Lady Hillary Clinton testified before a grand jury for her role in the Whitewater Scandal. Although neither she nor her husband President Bill Clinton were ever charged with any crime, the scandal about their involvement in the Whitewater Development Corporation, a failed business venture into real estate investments, put the Clintons' reputation at risk. Fourteen people were later convicted.

Also in 1996 the Siege of Sarajevo ended, having lasted 1,425 days. The Serbs finally withdrew their blockage leaving the city in the hands of the Croatians.

Football 'came home' when England hosted Euro 1996. The song chosen for the tournament was *Three Lions* by the Lightning Seeds, with music by the band's Ian Broudie and lyrics by comedians David Baddiel and Frank Skinner. England reached the semi-finals but were beaten by Germany who went on to beat the Czech Republic 2–1 in the final.

The Summer Olympics also took place. They were held in Atlanta, United States, with Mohammed Ali dramatically lighting the Olympic flame whilst clearly suffering from Parkinson's disease. Britain won a single gold medal, once again the reliable pairing of Matthew Pinsent and Steve Redgrave in the Men's Coxless Pair.

Famous people that died included François Mitterrand, President of France; Gene Kelly, actor and dancer; Ella Fitzgerald, jazz singer; and P. L. Travers, who was best known as the author of *Mary Poppins*.

1997

Passenger total 1,165,318.

Passenger increase of 60% on the previous year.
Number of flights 33,000, up 26%.

The airport topped the one million annual passenger throughput for the first time.

In April, some 20 years after the USA had deregulated air travel, Europe took the same path, ushering in a new era of cheaper flights for all. Any technically qualified airline in the European Union (plus Norway and Iceland) could from now on operate services from within any other European country. EasyJet advanced into France but no European mainland airline has offered point-to-point services within the UK.

Planning approval was granted to increase London City Airport movements at weekends. As part of its tenth birthday celebrations the airport put on a party for 4,000 local residents. London City Airport celebrated this anniversary with two souvenir publications.

New arrester beds, an important safety feature used to stop aircraft overrunning a runway, were incorporated at each end of the runway.

The Avro RJ70 arrived in the colours of Lufthansa CityLine.

Sabena overnights an aircraft at London City Airport – a first scheduled night-stop.

With the refurbishing of the original departure lounge new retail shops were added.

British Airways adopted a controversial new livery: a revised logo and around 20 different ethnic tailfins featuring art and designs of many countries around the world. Bob Ayling was Chief Executive when they were introduced but in 2001 incoming boss Rod Edington, an Australian, replaced them with the Chatham Dockyard Union flag already seen on Concorde. The tailfins were never seen at London City, since BA was absent from the airport during this period.

The first annual one million passengers called for a celebration.

Floral tributes to Princess Diana.

On 31 August the world was in mourning following the tragic untimely death of Princess Diana, in the well-documented car accident in the Pont de l'Alma road tunnel in Paris. Dodi Fayed, her boyfriend, together with Henri Paul, the driver, also died.

Around one million mourners lined the streets of London for the funeral at Westminster Abbey. Worldwide coverage was estimated to be 2.5 billion people. Famous figures from all over the globe came to pay their respects to the 'People's Princess' including Hillary Clinton, Nelson Mandela, Henry Kissinger and Luciano Pavarotti. Elton John performed a new version of his song *Candle in the Wind* at the service and Earl Spencer, Diana's brother gave a controversial eulogy.

On 5 September, one day before Princess Diana's funeral, Mother Teresa of Calcutta, Nobel Peace winner, passed away at the age of 87. In 1950 Teresa founded the Missionaries of Charity – a Roman Catholic religious congregation which went on to be active in 133 countries. Its work included managing homes for people dying of HIV/AIDS and other socially excluded illnesses such as running soup kitchens; dispensaries and mobile clinics as well as children's and family-counselling programmes; orphanages, and schools. However her passing was rather subdued because of the coverage received by the death of Diana. Mother Teresa was given a state funeral.

The British political system changed dramatically in 1997. On 1 May the Labour Party returned to power for the first time in 18 years, with Tony Blair becoming Prime Minister, in a landslide election victory. On 11 September both Scotland and Wales held referendums in favour of devolution which led to the formation of the Scottish and Welsh assemblies.

In the trial of British au pair Louise Woodward was found guilty of the shaking of eight-month old baby Matthew Eappen to death in the US. Media coverage of the case was intense, nowhere more so than in Britain. After appeal she was convicted of involuntary manslaughter and her sentence reduced to 279 days, the time she had spent in jail. Years later research seemed to substantiate her plea of innocence.

Israel handed Hebron, the last Israeli-controlled West Bank city, back to the Palestinians, in an important step for peace and after intense negotiations.

In business news 1997 was the year that Boeing and McDonnell Douglas completed its merger. The result created the world's second largest defence company and the largest aerospace group. The Douglas DC-9, by then renamed the MD80 series, became the Boeing 717.

In entertainment news Bloomsbury paid J. K. Rowling a paltry £2,500 for her book *Harry Potter and the Philosopher's Stone*. There was an initial print run of 500. (By 2017 it was estimated that 450 million copies had been sold.) Britain's other achievement was when Katrina and the Waves won the Eurovision Song Contest with *Love Shine a Light*. The classic film *Titanic* was released, with stars British Kate Winslet and American Leonardo DiCaprio, winning 11 Oscars and grossing $1.84 billion.

Famous deaths included Belfast born Chaim Herzog, President of Israel; James Stewart, actor; Gianni Versace, fashion designer (murdered by serial killer Andrew Cunanan); Viktor Frankl, neurologist and psychiatrist; Billy Bremner, Scottish footballer; and Michael Hutchence, Australian singer-songwriter.

1998

Passenger total 1,358,774.

Passenger increase of 17% on the previous year.
Number of flights 37,912, up 14%.

Signs were incorporated at both ends of the Connaught Bridge to the west of the airport saying 'Beware of low flying aircraft', not that anyone could miss the fact that there were aviation activities in the Royal Docks!

The North London Line to North Woolwich, stopping at Silvertown for London City Airport service, was reduced from three trains per hour to two, which did not go down well with the airport nor local residents. The station closed in 2004.

The airport staffing level had now reached 1,200.

31 March: The London Docklands Development Corporation passed into history. The local authority from now on would be the London Borough of Newham.

New routes to Gothenburg and Stockholm were said to have settled down well.

April: Nick Raynsford, Minister for London, opened the refurbished departure lounge. Approval was given for an increase in the maximum number of passenger flights.

The car park was enlarged and resurfaced.

Sheffield City Airport opened this year, virtually a copy of London City Airport, on disused industrial land in a city once known for its steel works. Flights were initiated by KLM and Aer Arann among others and included a London City route. (The highest passenger throughput came in 1999, but this was only 75,000 and by 2008 Sheffield City Airport had closed.) The Airport Manager for a period was John Horne who had held that post, on a temporary basis, at London City Airport.

BAe faith in LCY is rewarded with 146/Avro the most popular aircraft with airlines for over a decade.

Bill Clinton admits to an improper physical relationship with Monica Lewinsky, seen here at a London book signing.

Irish politics was a focus of British news. On 10 April the Good Friday Agreement was signed by all political parties in Northern Ireland and the Republic of Ireland, with the notable exception of the Democratic Unionist Party. The central issues of the Good Friday agreement were sovereignty, civil and cultural rights, decommissioning of weapons, justice and policing. On 22 May a referendum took place in each jurisdiction with both peoples supporting the agreement.

However, in response to the agreement, a car bomb exploded on 15 August in Omagh, County Tyrone, Northern Ireland, killing 29 people (including a woman pregnant with twins) as well as injuring some 220 others. It was carried out by the Real Irish Republican Army, a Provisional Irish Republican Army splinter group who opposed the IRA's ceasefire and the Good Friday Agreement. Nobody has been successfully convicted for the murders.

On 16 October British police placed General Augusto Pinochet, the Chilean dictator, under house arrest whilst he was receiving medical treatment. (He was held for a year and a half before being released in 2000, when he returned freely to Chile.) The house arrest was the first time that several European judges applied the principle of universal jurisdiction and declared themselves competent to judge crimes committed by former heads of state, despite local amnesty laws.

August was a busy month in terms of high profile American news stories. On 7 August the United States embassies in Dar es Salaam, Tanzania and Nairobi, Kenya were bombed, killing 224 people and injuring over 4,500. They were linked to terrorist Osama bin Laden, an exile of Saudi Arabia.

And then on 20 August in retaliation for the embassy bombings the United States military launched cruise missile attacks against alleged al-Qaeda camps in Afghanistan and a suspected chemical plant in Sudan. The al-Shifa pharmaceutical factory in Khartoum was destroyed in the attack.

On 19 August President Bill Clinton admitted in taped testimony that he had an 'improper physical relationship' with White House intern Monica Lewinsky. He also admitted before the nation that night in a nationally televised address that he 'misled people' about his sexual affair with Lewinsky. (He was later impeached for misleading the American people and then acquitted for any wrongdoing.)

In other stories, 120 countries voted to create a permanent International Criminal Court to prosecute individuals for genocide, crimes against humanity, war crimes, and the crime of aggression; the Kosovo war began between the then Federal Republic of Yugoslavia and a Kosovo Albanian rebel group with air support from the North Atlantic Treaty Organisation (NATO), and ground support from the Albanian army; the Second Congo War began with 3,900,000 people being killed before it ending in 2003, making it the bloodiest war, to date, since World War II. The war directly involved nine countries as well as approximately 20 separate armed groups.

In sport France won the FIFA World Cup on its home territory beating Brazil 3–0. The Winter Olympics took place in Japan. Team GB won a bronze medal in the bobsleigh event.

Famous people that passed away included Linda McCartney, activist and musician; Ted Hughes, poet; Catherine Cookson, author; Sonny Bono, singer and politician; Frank Sinatra, singer and actor; and Pol Pot, dictator.

1999

Passenger total 1,388,481.

This was a nominal increase on the previous year.
Number of flights 44,195, up 17%.

Suckling Airways arrived with a four times daily Dornier 228 service to Glasgow and also instigated a Dundee route. It was soon to become Scot Airways and graduated to the much sleeker Dornier 328.

The airport was gaining acceptance as a major gateway to London with the Jubilee Line extension to Stratford stopping at Canning Town. This was vital for the airport with just a short taxi ride or public transport connection to the London Underground.

A covered walkway was installed from the terminal building towards the car parks.

The airport administration moved from the terminal to the new City Aviation House. Originally it was in the area that is now the site of the main security search zone.

The Business Centre, a left turn at the top of the escalator to the first floor, was refurbished and on the technical front a new Instrument Landing System (ILS) was installed.

Proving a big success, the London City Airport Consultative Committee was now meeting four times a year. Normally the attendance was around 20 at the airport, with airlines and the local interests, the Association of British Travel Agents (ABTA) and the Docklands Forum always represented.

The actual passenger numbers only improved marginally.

Scot Airways took over Suckling (top) and replaced its Dornier 228s with the larger, faster and far more comfortable 328 (bottom).

TV presenter Jill Dando was murdered in a London street.

Three murder stories dominated British media – Dr Harold Shipman's 'Doctor Death' cruel murder of his patients, the London nail bombings and the murder of Jill Dando, the television presenter.

Britain was horrified to learn the previous year of the actions of Dr Harold Shipman, a General Practitioner, from Hyde, Greater Manchester. Police had discovered a pattern to his administering lethal doses of diamorphine, signing patients' death certificates, and then falsifying medical records to indicate they had been in poor health. His trial began on 5 October and he was found guilty of 15 murders (although it was later estimated that he murdered up to 250 patients) and he was given 15 recurrent life sentences.

During April David Copland, a Neo-Nazi, placed homemade nail bombs in holdalls that he left in public spaces over a 13-day period around London. The bombs placed in black, South Asian and gay communities resulted in three deaths and over 100 people being injured.

Queen Elizabeth's youngest son Prince Edward married Sophie Rhys-Jones on 19 June in St George's Chapel at Windsor Castle. He was created Earl of Wessex hours before the ceremony.

In international news in 1999 both the European Commission and the United States Federal Trade Commission approved the merger of Exxon and Mobil oil companies which created the Exxon Mobil Corporation, at that time the world's largest company.

Many events took place across the world for the entry of the 21st century. In London, attention focussed around Big Ben, the Millennium Dome and the fireworks display. This was called the 'River of Fire' and went along several miles of the Thames. In New York, a new Times Square Ball made of Waterford Crystal was commissioned and over two million attended celebrations. South Africa's Nelson Mandela lit a candle in his former cell at Robben Island at the stroke of midnight. The Eiffel Tower in Paris was the focal point of celebrations in France – 20,000 strobe lights were installed for the event and they still operate each night.

THE Sun

Jill Dando

1961-1999

ASSASSINATED

During 1999 the whole world was preparing for what became known as the 'Y2K problem' or the Millennium bug that was predicted to take place on 1 January 2000. Nothing happened – either due to the preparation for the event or because a problem would not have arisen in the first place.

The major British sporting achievement was Manchester United's defeat of the German side Bayern Munich 2–1 in the UEFA Champions League Final held in Barcelona, Spain.

On 26 April the much respected presenter of BBC's *Crimewatch*, Jill Dando, was murdered outside her home in Fulham in broad daylight. Barry George, a local who had a history of sexual offences, was charged with her murder but was later acquitted. As of July 2017 the crime remains unsolved.

Other famous deaths included Dusty Springfield, singer; Joe DiMaggio, baseball player and one-time husband of Marilyn Monroe; Ernie Wise, comedian; Lionel Bart, composer – most famous for the musical *Oliver*, Sir Alf Ramsey, World Cup winning football manager and Dirk Bogarde, actor.

2000

Passenger total 1,580,234.

Passenger increase of 14% on the previous year.
Number of flights 52,126, up 18%.

Real-time flight information became available online.

The Government announced £30 million funding for a DLR link to the airport and across the river to Woolwich Arsenal.

The one-millionth passenger of the year was welcomed earlier than ever before – 28 August. New baggage reclaim area completed.

ExCeL London opened, the western entrance exactly one mile, or 20 minutes' walk across the Connaught Bridge. The 473 bus ran every 15 minutes.

The Millennium Dome (now O2) opened on the Greenwich Peninsular amid scenes of transport chaos on New Year's Eve. The venue was of great benefit to the airport commercially with London City Airport taking a VIP box.

Ken Livingstone, an opponent of London City Airport, became the first Mayor of London.

Work started on the A13 road improvements (which were completed in 2004).

Planning applications were submitted for the Operational Improvements Programme for an increase in flight movements.

The Millennium Dome, now the O2, is a familiar sight for LCY passengers.

The Dome was doomed but the British Airways London Eye was a success.

There were three high profile cases of murder and manslaughter in Britain.

The first was the abduction and murder of eight-year-old Sarah Payne by a convicted paedophile, Roy Whiting, on 1 July. The *News of the World*, along with Sarah's parents, subsequently, lobbied for the rights of parents to have controlled access to the Sex Offenders Register. On 20 August controversy broke out when Tony Martin was sentenced to life imprisonment for the murder of a 16-year-old burglar he shot dead at his Norfolk farmhouse. His sentence was later reduced to manslaughter and the incident provoked a fierce debate over the right of homeowners to protect themselves and their property. Finally on 27 November, ten-year-old Damilola Taylor, a Nigerian schoolboy who lived in North Peckham, was murdered by a gang of boys. Several young boys were cleared of murder charges after a lengthy trial, and later two brothers were convicted of manslaughter.

The new Millennium saw the opening of several important structures in London. First came the Millennium or 'Wobbly' Bridge, linking Bankside with the City of London.

Soon after, with pedestrians feeling an unexpected swaying motion, it closed for two years whilst the problem was sorted out. Adjacent to the bridge the Tate Modern was revealed after a £134 million conversion of the Bankside Power Station. Also on the South Bank of the River Thames the London Eye opened – Europe's tallest ferris wheel and at the time offered the highest public viewing point in London. By 2015, 60 million people had visited it.

In political news on 4 May the independent candidate Ken Livingstone was elected Mayor of London, defeating the Conservative Party's Steve Norris.

Further afield on 26 March in Russia Vladimir Putin was elected as President.

On 7 November the United States held elections: Republican George W. Bush defeated Democrat Al Gore in a very tightly fought contest – the focus of the election eventually centred on the State of Florida with a dispute over how votes were counted. This election also saw Hillary Clinton become the Senator for New York – becoming the first former First Lady of the United States to win public office.

In business news, AOL purchased Time Warner for $164 billion, although final approval was not given until 2001. It was the largest ever corporate merger. Other business news saw BMW selling the Rover Group and The Royal Bank of Scotland taking over NatWest Bank after successfully defeating a rival offer by the Bank of Scotland.

In sport the Olympic Games were held in Sydney, Australia, with Team GB's Steve Redgrave winning his fifth consecutive gold for rowing. In football France become European Champions after defeating Italy 2–1 in the final; Wembley Stadium closed after 77 years to be completely reconstructed and Sven-Göran Eriksson, the Swedish coach, became the England football manager.

Famous people that passed away included Dame Barbara Cartland, novelist; Sir John Gielgud, actor; Lord (Robert) Runcie, Archbishop of Canterbury; Sir Robin Day, political broadcaster; Sir Stanley Matthews, footballer; Paula Yates, television presenter and Charles M. Schulz, creator of *Peanuts*.

2001

Passenger total 1,624,015.

Passenger increase of 3% on the previous year.
Number of flights 57,005, up 9%.

The new Arrivals Hall was completed.

Planning approval was granted for extension of the apron, a new runway link and a holding point.

The airport closed for two days following the terrorist attacks in New York on 11 September, with a knock-on effect resulting in a distinct drop in passenger numbers.

The Dassault Falcon 900EX executive jet among others was certificated for operations at the airport.

Embraer rolled out the E170 with Crossair CEO Moritz Suter at the ceremony which featured the aircraft painted in the Swiss airline's colour scheme on one side.

Above left: *LCY is not immune to the diversities of London's weather.*

Left: *October – the E Series rollout at São José dos Campos with Mauricio Botelho (left), Embraer President and Moritz Suter, Crossair CEO.*

Lord (Jeffrey) Archer, politician and writer, was found guilty of perjury and sentenced to four years.

On 11 September two US passenger planes were hijacked by members of the terrorist group al-Qaeda who flew the planes into the World Trade Towers. A third plane crashed into the Pentagon and a fourth was steered toward Washington DC but dived into a field near Shanksville, Pennsylvania, after its passengers tried to overcome the hijackers. The attacks killed 2,996 people, injured over 6,000 others, and caused at least $10 billion in property and infrastructure damage and $3 trillion in total costs. United States President George W. Bush subsequently declared a war on terror and Britain's Prime Minister Tony Blair pledged to stand 'Shoulder to Shoulder' with the United States. On 7 October, the United States, supported by the United Kingdom, invaded Afghanistan, with participation from other nations at a later date. The aim of the invasion was to dismantle al-Qaeda and remove the Taliban from power.

In Britain Marie-Thérèse Kouao and Carl Manning were found guilty of torturing and murdering eight-year-old Victoria Climbié. They were sentenced to life imprisonment. Many organisations including social services, police and the NHS were aware of her case and noticed signs of abuse before she died. The judge in the trial described it as 'blinding incompetence', that all failed to properly investigate the case and that little action was taken.

Also the foot and mouth crisis began. This epidemic saw 2,000 cases of the disease in farms across most of the British countryside. Over ten million cows and sheep were killed in an eventually successful attempt to halt the disease.

In politics on 7 June Tony Blair's Labour Party won a second successive General Election landslide victory. William Hague resigned as Conservative Party leader with Ian Duncan Smith taking his place. Later the next month, and still in politics, Jeffrey Archer, the politician and writer, was found guilty of perjury and perverting the course of justice during his libel trial.

On the international stage on 18 February Robert Hanssen was sentenced after being found to have been selling United States secrets to the Soviet Union. His activities were described by the Department of Justice's Commission for the Review of FBI Security Programs as 'possibly the worst intelligence disaster in US history'. At the G8 summit on 20–22 July in Genoa an anti-globalisation movement protest drew an estimated 200,000 demonstrators. Dozens were hospitalized following clashes with police and one demonstrator was shot dead.

On 2 December Enron, one of the world's largest electricity, natural gas, communications and pulp and paper companies, filed for bankruptcy. It was later revealed that its reported financial condition was sustained by institutionalized, systematic, and creatively planned accounting fraud. It was the largest bankruptcy in United States history.

Wikipedia, the free content encyclopaedia, went online and Kofi Annan, Head of the United Nations, gained the Nobel Peace Prize.

In sport Manchester United won the FA Premier League title for the third season in succession and Liverpool won the FA Cup.

Famous people who died included Stanley Kramer, film director and producer; Douglas Adams, English author; Jack Lemmon, actor and director; Mary Whitehouse, television campaigner; Sir Nigel Hawthorne, actor and George Harrison, musician and member of The Beatles.

2002

Passenger total 1,604,773.

Passenger decrease of 1% on the previous year.
Number of flights 56,102, also down 2%.

The most significant events were the airport celebrating its ten millionth passenger since the 1987 opening and the Government approval of the DLR extension to the airport. From then on, London City Airport began to appear on all the London Underground maps and truly became part of London's integrated transport network.

On the negative front, London City, like all airports, suffered from the aftermath of 9/11 with the loss of routes, in particular Inverness and Munich, which are not served at July 2017.

Work was completed on improvements at the west end of the apron including remote aircraft stands and a new fire simulator was commissioned.The noise insulation programme for the local community progressed well with 80% of the 872 properties treated with double glazing.

April: Air Wales started routes to Cardiff and Swansea three times weekdaily. (They did not last long but were resurrected in 2016 to Cardiff by Flybe.)

July: City Hall opened opposite the Tower of London, the first occupant was Ken Livingstone.

September: London City Airport owner Dermot Desmond opened the new Private Jet Centre for corporate aviation.

October: Wi-fi internet was introduced in the airport terminal (It is now free).

November: The airport celebrated its 15th birthday and valet parking was introduced.

All part of the LCY offering – free wi-fi and a concierge service.

On 7 November all but 2% of Gibraltar's population voted to stay British.

Queen Elizabeth had a very mixed year in 2002. Both her sister and her mother died but she celebrated her Golden Jubilee – the anniversary of 50 years of ascending the throne.

Princess Margaret, the Queen's sister, died at the age of 71 from a stroke and just seven weeks later her mother, Queen Elizabeth the Queen Mother passed away at the age of 101. The Queen Mother's state funeral was attended by presidents and royalty from all over the world. The Golden Jubilee celebrations included the Prom in the Palace concert, the Party at the Palace concert (which commenced with Queen Guitarist Brian May playing his arrangement of *God Save the Queen* from the roof of Buckingham Palace), and street parties throughout Britain.

Three murders of British children hit the headlines of British newspapers. Amanda Dowler, 13, went missing on her way home from school on 21 March and she was found dead on 18 September. (It was not until 2011 that Levi Bellfield, who was already in prison for two other murders, was found guilty of murdering Dowler.)

Holly Wells and Jessica Chapman, two ten-year-old girls from Soham, Cambridgeshire, went missing on 4 August and their bodies were found on 17 August. Ian Kevin Huntley, a caretaker at the local secondary school, was found guilty of their murders and sentenced to a minimum of 40 years in prison.

Other high profile British news stories included the case of Diane Petty, who suffered from the terminal illness motor neurone disease. She took her case to end her life by euthanasia to the European Court of Human Rights, but did not succeed and she died because of her illness later that year. On 10 May seven people died in the Potters Bar rail crash and on 7 November 98% of Gibraltar's population voted to stay a British overseas territory in a referendum.

In Europe the Euro was officially introduced in the Eurozone countries on 1 January. The former currencies of all the countries that used the Euro ceased to be legal tender on 28 February.

It was the year in which the war crimes trial of Slobodan Milošević began. The former President of Yugoslavia faced 66 counts of crimes against humanity, genocide and war crimes committed during the Yugoslav Wars and faced trial at the International Criminal Tribunal for the former Yugoslavia. However Milošević committed suicide before the trial ended and the court delivered a no verdict result.

In Israel a Palestinian suicide bomber killed 30 and injured 140 at a hotel in the South triggering Operation Defensive Shield – a large-scale counter-terrorism operation in the West Bank.

In sport the World Cup took place in South Korea and Japan. Brazil won the tournament beating Germany 2–0 and England reached the quarter finals. The Winter Olympics were held in Salt Lake City, Utah, and Manchester hosted the Commonwealth Games.

Famous people who died included Peggy Lee, singer and actress; Spike Milligan, comedian; Dudley Moore, actor; Billy Wilder, director and Jimmy Carter, President of the United States as well as Princess Margaret and Queen Elizabeth the Queen Mother.

2003

Passenger total 1,472,272.

Passenger decrease of 8% on the previous year.
Number of flights 52,563, down 6%.

Work was well under way with the airport DLR station, a situation regularly pointed out to potential airlines considering future services.

A new runway holding point and link allowed movements to go up to 32 per hour. Up to three aircraft could be held at the eastern end of the runway prior to take-off, or held after landing. With the runway at 1199m, compared with Gatwick's 3316m, the aircraft were actually moving for less than half the time, and passengers could regularly be landside in the terminal within ten minutes of touch down.

British Airways CitiExpress launched services from the airport, the airline an amalgamation of Brymon Airways, purchased by British Airways in 1993, and Gatwick-based City Flyer Express. Its first five routes were Edinburgh, Frankfurt, Geneva, Glasgow and Paris Charles de Gaulle.

Seventh Fun Day raised £24,000 for Richard House, a children's hospice in nearby Beckton.

Bill Bryce, the founder of Brymon Airways, died in New Zealand aged 70.

Corporate jet flights increased by 35% during the year carrying 16% more passengers although with executive aviation it is not the actual number travelling but the quality. Often the bizjets just carry two passengers.

Fire brigade in practice mode.

The London Congestion Charge was introduced.

On 20 March the United States, combined with forces from the United Kingdom, Australia and Poland, invaded Iraq in a mission called 'Operation Iraqi Freedom'. The stated aim of the war was 'to disarm Iraq of weapons of mass destruction, to end Saddam Hussein's support for terrorism, and to free the Iraqi people'. The coalition forces comprised 380,000 troops versus Iraq's 375,000. The mission consisted of 21 days of major combat but finally ended on 1 May. In part it could be said that the mission completed its aims with coalition forces toppling the Government of Saddam Hussein and capturing the key cities of a large nation in only 21 days.

The need for the war was not universally accepted. Andrew Gilligan of the BBC reported that the Government knew that its claim that Iraq could deploy weapons of mass destruction within 45 minutes was dubious. Gilligan's key source for the report, David Kelly, a weapons expert, was brought to answer questions before the House of Commons Foreign Affairs Select Committee and was aggressively questioned by Members of Parliament. Kelly faced a huge amount of pressure and went on to commit suicide. The Government then opened the Hutton Inquiry into the circumstances of his death and following its publication the BBC's Director-General, Greg Dyke, Chairman of the Board of Governors, Gavyn Davies, and Andrew Gilligan, resigned.

There were worldwide protests against the invasion and almost 3,000 demonstrations took place throughout the world. Around 36 million people took part in protests including two million in London.

In other British news Sally Clark, who had been previously found guilty of murdering her two new-born sons, was freed from prison after her conviction was overturned. It was found that her children died of Sudden Infant Death Syndrome. The Congestion Charge was introduced on 17 February covering the approximate area of the London Inner Ring Road. The Charge was £5, when it was introduced.

Concorde touched down for the last time; Roger Short, the British Consul-General in Turkey was killed by a truck bombing in Istanbul along with at least 27 people; Ian Carr, who had 89 previous convictions (including causing death by dangerous driving), admitted causing the death by dangerous driving of a six-year-old girl. Den Watts (played by Leslie Grantham) returned to the television soap *EastEnders* 14 years after the character was supposedly killed off.

European political news focussed on referendums in the Czech Republic, Estonia Hungary, Latvia, Lithuania, Malta, Poland, Slovakia and Slovenia. All countries voted yes to the referendum and became members of the EU in 2004. Bulgaria, Estonia, Latvia, Lithuania, Romania, Slovakia and Slovenia also voted on whether to become members of NATO and were admitted the following year – it was the largest expansion of the organization.

Sports news saw AC Milan win the UEFA Champions League when they beat Juventus in a penalty shootout at Old Trafford. England became the rugby world champions defeating the hosts Australia 20–17 in extra time.

Famous people who died included Maurice Gibb, singer from the Bee Gees, Gregory Peck, actor; Katherine Hepburn, actress; Bob Hope, comedian-actor; Lord (Roy) Jenkins, politician; Sir Denis Thatcher, husband to Prime Minister Lady (Margaret) Thatcher and Bob Monkhouse, entertainer.

2004

Passenger total 1,684,545.

Passenger increase of 14% on the previous year.
Number of flights 60,500, up 15%.

Custom House and Prince Regent stations opened at either end of ExCeL London with the completion of the Beckton extension. This offered another public gateway to the airport, a short bus or taxi ride away.

The airport celebrated its one millionth Edinburgh passenger since service began in 1996. March was a record month for passenger numbers with over 150,000, an improvement of 20% over the previous March.

The VLM Manchester service was a great success, at least six rotations weekdaily with a Fokker 50, nearly 60% load factor and 133,000 passengers. The same airline also served Liverpool with about half the number of travellers. (Both these routes failed in later years due to the much-improved Virgin train services to north-west England.)

Leeds Bradford Airport became a destination flown by bmi.

Corporate aircraft movements reached a record high of 14,000.

By 2004 the DLR extension to the airport was well under way.

Norman Foster's 'Gherkin' arrived in the City of London.

Ken Bigley, a British civil engineer, was kidnapped in the al-Mansour district of Baghdad, along with his colleagues Jack Hensley and Eugene Armstrong and was beheaded. Later in the year Margaret Hassan, an Irish-born aid worker who had worked in Iraq for many years, was abducted and murdered by unidentified kidnappers.

Also in 2004 Lord Butler published the findings from his inquiry into the intelligence used to make the decision to go to war in Iraq. The report said the intelligence used to justify the war was now in doubt. The Iraq Survey Group also published its findings and concluded there had been no stockpiles of weapons of mass destruction in Iraq.

It was also the year that Norman Foster's 'The Gherkin', the easily identifiable skyscraper in the City of London, opened.

Politics had a flamboyant year in 2004: A Fathers4Justice protester almost managed to breach Buckingham Palace security dressed as Batman and pro-foxhunter groups staged protests in the House of Commons – the former threw purple powder at the Prime Minister at Question Time and the latter managed to suspend parliament. Also in 2004 in May Tony Blair led the Labour Party to victory in a United Kingdom General Election and Ken Livingstone was re-elected as the Mayor of London.

On Sunday 6 June Heads of State – including Queen Elizabeth and President George W. Bush – and thousands of war veterans gathered in France to mark the 60th anniversary of the D-Day invasion of Nazi-occupied Europe.

In international news the Israeli Air Force killed Sheikh Ahmed Yassin, Hamas spiritual leader and Abdel Aziz al-Rantisi, his second in command, in two separate missions; the United States formally handed back Iraqi sovereignty; Afghanistan had its first democratic election, won by Hamid Karzai, an independent. Over 300 people, more than half of them children, died at a school siege in Beslan, in the Russian Federation.

At the end of the year on Boxing Day a tsunami in the Indian Ocean killed 230,000–280,000 people in 14 countries, and inundated coastal communities with waves up to 100 feet high. It was one of the deadliest natural disasters in recorded history. Indonesia was the hardest-hit country, followed by Sri Lanka, India, and Thailand. The World Bank initially estimated the amount of aid needed at $5 billion and by 1 January 2005 over $1.8 billion had been pledged.

There were two significant sporting events – the UEFA Cup and the Summer Olympics. The UEFA Cup was held in Portugal. Unexpectedly Greece won the cup beating Portugal in the final. England reached the quarter finals. The Olympic Games were held in Athens. Team GB won nine gold medals, nine silver and 12 bronze including golds for Bradley Wiggins, Kelly Holmes and Chris Hoy. American swimmer Michael Phelps won a record six gold and two bronze medals, becoming the first athlete to win eight medals in a non-boycotted Olympics.

Famous people that died included Estée Lauder, the American cosmetics entrepreneur, Ronald Reagan, President of the United States and actor; John Peel, broadcaster; Christopher Reeve, actor and campaigner; Yasser Arafat, Palestinian leader and Marlon Brando, actor.

2005

Passenger total 1,997,922.

Passenger increase of 19% on the previous year.
Number of flights 70,912, up 17%.

Luxair launched jet services using the 37-seat Embraer ERJ-135 aircraft, VLM opened up the Isle of Man and SAS arrived from Copenhagen. Another new airline was SUN-AIR as a British Airways franchise to Copenhagen.

Euromanx to Galway was another speculative route this year which in three months carried just 10,000 passengers at an average 35% load factor.

An inquiry opened into the Thames Gateway Bridge – it was never to happen.

Work started on Woolwich Arsenal extension of DLR prior to the completion of a new station called King George V, much nearer the dock than the old North Woolwich terminus.

A plaque was unveiled at the redeveloped Heron Quays DLR station to commemorate the trial Dash 7 landings there in 1982 (later moved).

During the summer and autumn test trains began to run on the DLR extension as far as the temporary terminus at King George V.

The airport celebrated the arrival of the one millionth passenger using the Rotterdam service.

With the start of the winter season in October, 13 airlines were serving six domestic points out of a total 23 destinations.

The airport is finally recognized by the Mayor of London, Ken Livingstone officially opening the DLR London City Airport station on Tuesday 6 December. Timings were seven minutes to Canning Town, with connections to the Jubilee Line, and 22 minutes to Bank, for the Northern and Central Lines.

Press off first. Darwin Airlines arrives from Bern, Switzerland. In 2017 the aircraft operates for Swiss airline Skywork to LCY.

The London bombings.

This year was marked by the 7 July London bombings. The attack – a series of coordinated suicide bombings on London's public transport system – took place during the morning rush hour. Three bombs exploded on different Underground trains almost simultaneously and a fourth bomb exploded on a bus an hour later. Fifty-two people were killed and over 700 were injured.

On 21 July there were further attacks on the Underground. However, there were no injuries. London was at this stage on a hyper sense of alert and on 22 July the Metropolitan Police shot and killed Jean Charles de Menezes, believed by them – mistakenly – to be a suicide bomber.

On 10 February Prince Charles married Camilla Parker Bowles at a civil ceremony at Windsor Guildhall. She took the title HRH Duchess of Cornwall. In politics on 5 May the Labour Party, led by Tony Blair, won its third successive election, with a reduced majority of 66. The Conservative leader, Michael Howard, resigned and David Cameron was subsequently elected as leader.

On 11 July Littlewoods disappeared from the British high street, its 119 stores converted to Primark. The chain was also in the process of closing 126 Index outlets with the loss of 3,200 jobs, and sold the remaining 44 Index sites to Argos.

Hurricane Katrina was the big news story in the USA. The storm, in August, was the third most intense measured storm in United States history. It affected Florida, New Orleans, Louisiana, Mississippi, Alabama and other areas including Cuba and Canada. At least 1,245 people died; hundreds of thousands of people were displaced and it caused an estimated $108 billion in damage. The response to the disaster has been highly criticised and officials, even including President George W. Bush, seemed unaware of just how bad things were in New Orleans and elsewhere.

In other international news on 2 April Pope John Paul II passed away. The requiem Mass was said to have set world records both for attendance and number of heads of state present at a funeral – four Kings, five Queens and at least 70 Presidents and Prime Ministers attended and an estimated in excess of four million mourners gathering in

and around Vatican City. Between 250,000 and 300,000 watched the event from within the Vatican's walls. Pope Benedict XVI succeeded him.

The Danish newspaper *Jyllands-Posten* on 30 September published controversial drawings of Muhammad. This sparked outrage and violent riots by Muslims around the world resulting in more than 200 deaths, attacks on Danish and other European diplomatic missions and a major international boycott.

Other news included commemorations held on 27 January to mark the 60th anniversary of the liberation of Auschwitz concentration camp; the Kyoto Protocol, extending the UN Framework Convention on Climate Change, came into effect on 16 February; the largest ever passenger plane – the Airbus A380 – made its maiden voyage in a test flight on 27 April from Toulouse Blagnac; Israel withdrew from the Gaza strip in August; 1,000 people died in a stampede during a religious festival in Iraq on 31 August; Angela Merkel assumed office as the first female Chancellor of Germany on 22 November.

In sport Liverpool won their fifth European Cup; London was chosen to host the 2012 Olympic Games in a dramatic occasion in Singapore. The England cricket team won The Ashes, with the final match at The Oval.

Famous people that died included Arthur Miller, playwright and sometime husband of Marilyn Monroe; Simon Wiesenthal, Austrian Holocaust survivor and Nazi hunter; Sir Edward Heath and Lord (James) Callaghan, both Prime Ministers of the United Kingdom; George Best, footballer; and Ronnie Barker, comedian.

2006

Passenger total 2,377,318.

Passenger increase up 19% on the previous year.
Number of flights 79,616, up 12%.

New London Mayor Boris Johnson called for the closure of London City Airport if Crossrail (Elizabeth Line) were to happen. He was a supporter of an estuary airport.

A new airline arrival was Eastern Airways from Newcastle with a four times daily service.

Silvertown for London City Airport had already closed but the new DLR station actually at the airport more than compensated for it. With outbound passengers learning about the DLR, and inbound travellers seeing for themselves already 40% of the airport's traffic was using the light railway.

January: Annual passenger total reached rolling two million.

April: Airport Master Plan published for consultation.

May: An Airbus A318 undertook a series of flights to check the feasibility of landing at the 5.5-degree glide slope needed as a noise abatement requirement, rather than the 3 degrees required at a regular airport. This was by far the largest aircraft to have flown in, but with a 32-seat all-Business Class layout it would be unable to take off with a full fuel load. Planned for a service to New York's Kennedy Airport, a refuelling stop would be required at Shannon Airport on the west coast of Ireland.

May: Twentieth anniversary of the laying of the terminal foundation stone by Prince Charles.

With the start of the winter season in October, 13 airlines were serving six domestic points out of a total 23 destinations. There were an additional eight 'summer only' routes.

November: Global Infrastructure Partners (GIP), a newly created investment fund incorporated in New York, teamed up with American International Group (AIG) to acquire the airport from Dermot Desmond for around £750 million. (As the lead investor AIG was later to acquire from BAA Plc both Edinburgh and Southampton airports.)

From this entrance to LCY you can see the Elizabeth Line about 130 yards down Parker Street.

South Korean Ban Ki-moon, the new Secretary-General of the United Nations.

The British police were on high alert for terrorism, and in one mission they foiled a plot to bring down at least ten aircraft bound for North America.

Also in 2006 Alexander Litvinenko, a former Russian secret service officer living in the United Kingdom, suddenly fell ill and was hospitalised in what was established as a case of poisoning by radioactive polonium-210. He became the first known victim of lethal polonium-210-induced acute radiation syndrome.

In other British news £53 million was stolen from a Securitas depot at Tonbridge, Kent, in the largest cash robbery in British crime history. The BBC announced that *Grandstand*, its flagship sports television programme, would be phased out after nearly 50 years on air and the BBC's *Top Gear* presenter Richard Hammond was seriously injured whilst driving a Vampire turbojet drag racing car at up to 314 miles per hour as part of a planned feature for the programme.

There was much news coming out of the Middle East in 2006. Israel once again found itself dealing with militants on two fronts, from the south by Hamas, and in the north with Hezbollah. In July, a 34-day conflict between Israel and the Hezbollah military saw battle between Israel and Hezbollah on the Lebanese border. The war was provoked after the kidnapping of two Israeli soldiers, subsequently Israel launched an offensive which included a naval blockade. The war ended after the United Nations brokered an agreement. A campaign was launched at the end of June against Palestinian militants in Gaza as a response to the capture of Israeli soldier Gilad Shalit as well as the Palestinian firing of Qassam rockets into Southern Israel. A shaky ceasefire was agreed at the end of November. Figures estimate that seven Israelis and 402 Palestinians were killed. Also in 2006 the former President of Iraq, Saddam Hussein, was sentenced to death by hanging by the Iraqi Special Tribunal. His execution took place on 30 December.

Other stories from the Middle East included a stampede during the last day at the Hajj in which at least 362 pilgrims were killed; an Egyptian passenger ferry, sunk in the Red Sea off the coast of Saudi Arabia, killing over 1,000 people and in Iraq the militant leader Abu Musab al-Zarqawi was killed in an air raid. He had been considered the figurehead of the Sunni insurgency and blamed for thousands of deaths.

In British-related Middle Eastern news peace activist Norman Kember was rescued in Baghdad by a multi-national force including the SAS. In Afghanistan an RAF Nimrod crashed and 14 personnel were killed in Britain's worst single military loss since the Falklands War.

In other worldwide news South Korean Ban Ki-moon was elected as the new Secretary-General of the United Nations, succeeding Kofi Annan and Montenegro declared independence from Serbia after a referendum.

In sport the Winter Olympics were held in Turin, Italy. Great Britain won one silver medal. The FIFA World Cup took place in Germany with England reaching the quarter-finals when they lost on penalties to Portugal after a goalless draw. The FIFA Cup was won by Italy who beat France on penalties. After the World Cup, Steve McClaren took over from Sven-Göran Eriksson as England manager.

Famous people that died in 2006 included John Kenneth Galbraith, economist; Aaron Spelling, television producer, P.W. Botha, State President of South Africa; Milton Friedman, Nobel economist; Robert Altman, film director; Augusto Pinochet, President of Chile and Gerald R. Ford, President of the United States.

2007

Passenger total 2,928,920.

Passenger increase of 23% on the previous year.
Number of flights 91,489, up 15%.

Roy Griffins appointed Chairman of London City Airport by the new owners. In fact it was a return for Roy who, as Private Secretary to Paul Channon, then Secretary of State for Transport, had accompanied Queen Elizabeth for the official opening of the airport. (After a 30-year involvement in the airport he retired in 2017.)

Bill Lindsell, essentially a lifetime Mowlem man, director and supporter of the airport, passed away on 1 March aged 77.

January: Airport given permission temporarily to vary the daily air transport movement limits but without changing the overall annual total.

In January, AirOne, an Italian Lufthansa partner and competitor to Alitalia, commenced services non-stop from Rome Fiumicino with the ubiquitous BAe 146. (Very soon it would be amalgamated into troubled Alitalia.)

March: BA Cityflyer was unveiled as a subsidiary of British Airways under its own Air Operators Certificate (AOC). British Airways owned 49% of Brymon at the time of the very first scheduled flight into London City Airport and had previously also operated at the airport as BA CitiExpress and BA Connect.

May: Airport confirms a £19 million contract for East Apron Extension project.

July: The Red Bull Air Race took place, not using the airport but a special runway on the north side of the dock.

August: Airport applied for planning permission to raise the limit on the number of flights to 120,000.

18 August: A SWISS Avro RJ 100 had what was described as a 'heavy landing' but was able to taxi to a stand. The structural damage was considered repairable but could not be completed within the airport confines. The aircraft was floated on a barge to the Royals Business Park opposite the Albert Dock from the airport. A temporary hangar was erected, the work undertaken and the process reversed nine weeks later when the aircraft returned into service. (See Chapter Eleven 'Heavy SWISS Landing')

December: Air France/KLM acquired VLM.

The extended apron is completed.

Gordon Brown (left) became UK PM – he was to last until 2010 – here seen with his predecessor Tony Blair.

The New Year blew in with storms and gales across the United Kingdom. Eleven people died, 100,000 people were left without electricity, over 200 flights were cancelled, rail speed restrictions were enforced and sections of the motorway were shut as gusts of wind of up to 99 miles per hour swept the country.

Four-year-old Madeleine McCann went missing on 3 May from her bed in a holiday apartment in Praia da Luz, a resort in the Algarve region of Portugal. Her distraught parents, Kate and Gerry McCann, mounted a high-profile campaign to ensure she was rarely out of the news in the weeks, months and years that followed. As of July 2017 she has not been found.

There were several major British media news stories in 2007. In January *News of the World's* royal editor Clive Goodman was jailed for four months when he pleaded guilty to intercepting voicemail messages from the Royal Household. Also in January protests were held in India and the United Kingdom against the British series of *Celebrity Big Brother* after celebrities were racially abusive to fellow housemate Bollywood star Shilpa Shetty. In March BBC correspondent Alan Johnston – the only international journalist working in Gaza at the time – was kidnapped. He was released after four months.

In other British news, on 23 March elements of the Iranian navy forcibly detained 15 British Royal Navy personnel. The HMS *Cornwall* crew members were on routine patrol in the Shatt al-Arab waterway when they were taken. Just less than two weeks later they returned home, unharmed.

In British politics on 27 June Gordon Brown became Prime Minister and Leader of the Labour Party after Tony Blair stood down after ten years in the role.

In Europe, Bulgaria and Romania joined the European Union and Slovenia joined the Eurozone. The Czech Republic, Estonia, Hungary, Latvia, Lithuania, Malta, Poland, Slovakia and Slovenia also joined the Schengen border-free zone. Together with the 2004 enlargement, it is considered part of the fifth wave of enlargement of the EU.

The year saw the start of the US subprime mortgage crisis, a nationwide banking emergency. It was triggered by the collapse in home value prices after a housing bubble, leading to mortgage foreclosures and the devaluation of housing-related securities.

In other international news, on 13 January a 27-year-old Cambodian girl was found living wild in the jungle after disappearing when she was eight years old. On 27 December Benazir Bhutto was assassinated by a suicide bomber after leaving an election rally in Rawalpindi. She was leader of the opposition at the time, but had previously been Prime Minister of Pakistan. At least 20 other people died in the attack and several more were injured. Bhutto had previously survived a similar attempt on her life that killed at least 139 people, after her return from exile two months earlier.

Famous people that died included Sidney Sheldon, author and screenwriter; Boris Yeltsin, first President of the Russian Federation; Luciano Pavarotti, Italian tenor and Anita Roddick, entrepreneur and founder of The Body Shop.

2008

Passenger total 3,271,716.

Passenger increase of 12% on the previous year.
Number of flights 94,763, up 4%.

The list of airlines was impressive: Air One, Austrian, BA CityFlyer, CityJet (Air France), KLM, Lufthansa, Luxair, SAS, SWISS.

British Airways announced an order for six Embraer E170 aircraft and five E190 for use at London City Airport.

February: Following the trials held in 2006, British Airways announced a new service to New York. A pair of special Airbus A318 were acquired and certificated with not only special wing flaps and spoilers required for a 5.5-degree landing angle, but also the technical equipment for the non-stop crossing from New York's JFK airport. As part of the British Airways' mainline operation, separate from Cityflyer, the publicity generated helped raise the profile of BA Cityflyer and the airport considerably.

March: Cityflyer opened new routes to Amsterdam, Barcelona, Nice, plus Warsaw which was short-lived.

May: An enlarged departure lounge was opened to passengers and the East Apron Extension project completed ready for the A318.

September: AIG sold its share (25%) of the airport to Highstar Capital with the balance owned by Global Infrastructure Partners (GIP).

October: Newham Council approved in principle the airport's application to raise the limit on the number of flights.

26 October: Airport celebrated the 21st anniversary of its opening for flights.

November: The Mayor of London abandons Thames Gateway Bridge and DLR Barking Extension projects.

December: Work was started on Phase 2 of the refurbishment of the departure lounge.

Chairman Roy Griffins (left) and Chief Executive Richard Gooding celebrating 21 years of LCY in 2008.

Incumbent Ken Livingstone (left) virtually self-destructs allowing Boris Johnson to become Mayor of London.

Continuing from the 2007 subprime mortgage crisis stock markets around the world plunged amid growing fears of a United States recession. The Lehman Brothers bank filed for bankruptcy in the USA, and in the United Kingdom HBOS merged with Lloyds (completed 2009) to prevent its collapse. The British Government announced a rescue package worth some £500 billion for United Kingdom banks with, in the end, only Lloyds (finally fully privatised 2017) and Royal Bank of Scotland participating. The Northern Rock Bank was nationalised.

There were two unusual cases of missing people that hit British headlines in 2008. A major investigation was launched on 19 February when nine-year-old Shannon Louise Matthews went missing. The girl's mother, Karen Matthews, and her boyfriend, Michael Donovan, had hidden Shannon with the aim of collecting reward money for her when she had been found. Both Mathews and Donovan were later sentenced to eight years imprisonment.

On 1 December John Darwina, a former probation officer, who was last seen paddling out to sea in his canoe in 2002, walked into a police station claiming no memory of the last five years. It then emerged that together with his wife, Anne, he had faked his death in order to claim life insurance. He and his wife Anne were later both convicted for fraud.

In other British news Conservative Boris Johnson became Mayor of London on 4 May, beating the incumbent Ken Livingstone; BBC Radio's *Russell Brand Show* came to an abrupt end on 18 October after airing a series of prank phone calls to the actor Andrew Sachs by Jonathan Ross and the show's host. On 19 December MFI, the furniture retailer ceased trading, closing all 111 of its stores and leaving its 1,400 workforce redundant.

Austria hit the headlines when it transpired that 73-year-old Josef Fritzl had imprisoned his daughter in a cellar for 24 years and fathered her seven children. He also admitted burning the body of a baby that died at the house in Amstetten, Lower Austria. He was sentenced to life imprisonment.

The international financial crisis hit Iceland hard and involved the default of all three of the country's major privately-owned commercial banks in late 2008, following their difficulties in refinancing their short-term debt and a run on deposits in the Netherlands and the United Kingdom. Relative to the size of its economy, Iceland's systemic banking collapse was the largest experienced by any country in economic history. The crisis led to a severe economic depression in 2008–2010 and significant political unrest.

In American politics Barack Obama won the USA Presidential election, becoming the first African-American President of the United States. He was elected over Republican John McCain.

In summer 2008 the Olympics took place in Beijing, China. Team GB won 19 gold, 13 silver and 15 bronze medals – the best performance for a Great Britain team in a century. Cyclist Chris Hoy became the first British athlete in 100 years to win three gold medals at a single Olympic Games. In the Paralympics Britain finished second in the medal table, behind host nation China, winning 42 gold medals including medals for the swimmer Eleanor Simmonds and the cyclist Sarah Storey.

Famous people that died included Sir Edmund Hillary, explorer; Arthur C. Clarke, author; Yves Saint Laurent, fashion designer; Paul Newman, actor and Harold Pinter, playwright.

2009

Passenger total 2,802,296.

Passenger decrease 14% on the previous year.
Number of flights 75,678, down 20%.

The direction of magnetic north decreases by approximately eight minutes of a degree every 12 months. It is minimal. On 2 July the airport's runway designators changed from 28/10 to 27/09 which should be good for 50 years. Signage and markings had to be changed overnight and also a comprehensive list of documents.

A major boost for the airport was the G20 Summit held at the nearby ExCeL London with a great deal of traffic to and from Brussels, before, during and after the one day event. Coupled with the high profile British Airways' New York JFK service it helped to ensure that the numbers at London City Airport were at least reasonable during a difficult period with passenger numbers in decline.

January: Train services started on the Woolwich Arsenal extension of the DLR.

A new service to Billund in Denmark, the home of Lego, commenced on 19 January, operated by SUN-AIR. On the same day Aer Arann launched flights to the Isle of Man using an ATR42 aircraft. This destination was already served by VLM which replaced the defunct Euromanx service.

March/April: Embraer E190 visited London City Airport for validation trials.

April: Air Southwest, the successor to Brymon Airways, introduced services from Plymouth and Newquay.

July: Airport was granted planning permission to raise the limit on the number of flights.

September: British Airways launched a high profile Airbus A318 business class service to New York JFK putting London City Airport very much on the international airport map. Passengers in the British Airways' Kennedy lounge always looked up when the route was called, and some asked to change their London entry point.

October: The airport's 75% owner Global Infrastructure Partners agreed to purchase London Gatwick Airport.

December: British Airways announces new services to Palma (Majorca) and Ibiza from May 2010.

Two arrivals. (top) The first Embraer 170, and (bottom) destined for only a short time, Air Southwest from Plymouth.

Pop legend Michael Jackson died.

The fallout of the financial crisis continued to hit Britain hard in 2009. The Bank of England cut interest rates to 1.5% – the lowest level in its 315-year history; the Royal Bank of Scotland announced annual losses totalling £24.1 billion – the biggest loss in British corporate history. The Government took a controlling stake, reported to be 65%, in the troubled Lloyds Banking Group with guarantees that toxic loans totalling £260 billion would be insured by the Government as part of the deal.

In other British news – on 5 January Waterford Wedgwood, makers of the famous Wedgwood pottery, entered administration; on 25 February Conservative leader David Cameron's six-year-old son Ivan, who had cerebral palsy and epilepsy, died at a hospital in London; on 16 May the Speaker of the House of Commons, Michael Martin, resigned over his part in the expenses row and on 22 June John Bercow replaced him. On 23 July the Government launched the National Pandemic Flu Service across England, a website and phone line allowed people who thought they had the H1N1 virus to bypass the NHS to obtain antiviral drugs. The website crashed within hours of its launch due to the overwhelming demand. November was the wettest calendar month since records began in 1910.

In American news, on 15 January pilots Chesley Sullenberger and Jeffrey Skiles successfully guided US Airways Flight 1549 into the Hudson River after it struck a flock of Canada geese and consequently lost all engine power. The pilots made the very quick decision to ditch in the river rather than attempt to land at a New York airport. All 155 people aboard were rescued by nearby boats and there were few serious injuries. In 2016 the film *Sully*, starring Tom Hanks and directed by another Hollywood 'Great' Clint Eastwood, portrayed the story.

On 25 June, the pop legend Michael Jackson died on the eve of his 51st birthday, after suffering from cardiac arrest. The Los Angeles County Coroner later concluded that his death was a homicide as shortly before his death Jackson had been administered drugs by his personal physician, Conrad Murray. He was convicted of involuntary manslaughter and served a two-year prison sentence. Jackson's death triggered a global outpouring of grief and as the news spread quickly online, it caused websites to slow down and crash from user overload, and put unprecedented strain on social media websites. A live broadcast of his memorial service in Los Angeles was watched by over one billion people.

In sport in 2009 Great Britain's Jenson Button won the Formula One Drivers' Championship driving a McClaren.

Other famous people that died included Natasha Richardson, actress; Keith Floyd, chef; Patrick Swayze, actor; Sir Bobby Robson, manager of England's football team; Wendy Richards, actress; Jade Goody, reality television star.

2010

Passenger total 2,793,813.

Passenger decrease 0.3% on the previous year.
Number of flights 67,917, down 10%.

A major terminal expansion was underway, taking away the atrium style check-in area by roofing it over with a first floor. This allowed an increase in the size of the security area and ultimately create the large airside lounge and retail concourse.

February: Not an airline arrival this time but sandwich specialist Pret A Manger opened up a retail unit. Oddly named airline Fly Baboo came in from Geneva with Bombardier Q400 aircraft but failed a year later, being taken over by Darwin Airlines.

Air Southwest also cancelled services to Plymouth and Newquay.

April: The eruption of Icelandic volcano Eyjafjallajökull caused the closure of most of European regulated airspace 15–20 April, which had knock-on effects for all European airline operations.

May: London City Airport was forced to admit that it was becoming a sensible holiday getaway point from East London with the introduction of Cityflyer flights to Ibiza and Majorca. While the original concept of a business traveller airport still prevailed, leisure traffic was on the increase.

July: It was in some ways the end of an era when the last Avro RJ100 left the British Airways fleet. The aircraft was originally produced as the Hawker Siddeley (HS) 146 in 1981 and was to become the best-selling British jet airliner of all time with 387 produced. (In 2017 CityJet is the main London City Airport operator of the Avro and says it will continue with the aircraft until at least 2020). See The British Aerospace 146/Avro RJ – in Chapter Ten.

October: Airport welcomed its 30 millionth passenger.

November: A study shows that the airport contributed £0.5 billion per year to the local economy.

The atrium is filled in. Compare with page 78.

David Cameron arrives at Downing Street.

Ash from the volcanic eruption of Eyjafjallajökull in Iceland caused a shut-down of airports throughout Europe in 2010. IATA stated that the total loss for the airline industry was around $1.7 billion. Airport closures lasted six days. This was the United Kingdom's longest airspace restriction in living memory.

The British elections led to a hung parliament with the Conservative Party 19 short of a majority. After negotiation the Conservatives and the Liberal Democrats formed a coalition with the Prime Minister David Cameron and David Clegg as his Lib Dem deputy. Gordon Brown, the Labour leader, resigned and was replaced by Ed Miliband after he beat his brother, David, in a leadership battle.

There was an important announcement with the news that Prince William was to marry long-term girlfriend Kate Middleton in 2011. Other historic British news was that Birmingham-based confectionery giant Cadbury was taken over by American rival Kraft Foods in an £11.5 billion deal.

In international news the publication of thousands of United States Embassy cables by WikiLeaks, the online publisher of anonymous, covert and classified material, continued when it leaked to the public over 90,000 internal reports about the US-led involvement in the War in Afghanistan from 2004 to 2010. However the focus of the story shifted later to its founder, Julian Assange, who was fighting extradition to Sweden over sex assault allegations.

Two major incidents happened in Chile – an earthquake and a miraculous saving of miners trapped underground. The 8.8-magnitude earthquake on 27 February triggered a tsunami over the Pacific and killed at least 525. It was estimated that the earthquake cost the Chilean economy $15–30 billion. On 5 August Chile was again on the international front pages when a cave-in at the troubled 121-year-old San José copper-gold mine left 33 men trapped 2,300ft underground. After 69 days, and an international effort involving technology from NASA, all 33 were saved. The rescue offered some respite to a people recovering from the earthquake disaster.

In other news on 12 January a devastating earthquake struck Haiti, claiming well over 100,000 lives and leaving more than one million people homeless; on 3 April Apple launched its first iPad; and on 20 September the 'Flash Crash' – a trillion-dollar stock market crash – occurred over 36 minutes, initiated by a series of automated trading programs in a feedback loop.

In sport England's bid to host the 2018 FIFA World Cup failed having attracted only two votes; FIFA awarded the tournament to Qatar instead but allegations of corruption arose; the 2010 Winter Olympics were held in Vancouver, Canada, and the FIFA World Cup was held in South Africa, and won by Spain, with the runner-up being the Netherlands. England was knocked out by Germany in the opening round.

Famous people that died included Tony Curtis, actor; Alexander McQueen, fashion designer; Michael Foot, politician; Juan Antonio Samaranch, President International Olympic Committee; Dennis Hopper, actor; and Leslie Nielsen, actor and comedian.

2011

Passenger total 3,005,759.

Passenger increase 7.6% on the previous year.
Number of flights 68,100, up 0.3%.

With preparations for the London Olympics in full swing the airport broke the annual three-million passenger barrier for the first time. When one considers that the largest aircraft operating from London City carried only 112 passengers this was a fine effort putting it above Belfast City and closing fast with Aberdeen, both capable of accommodating much larger planes.

Luxury travel down to the Private Jet Centre, and also from time to time to ExCeL London.

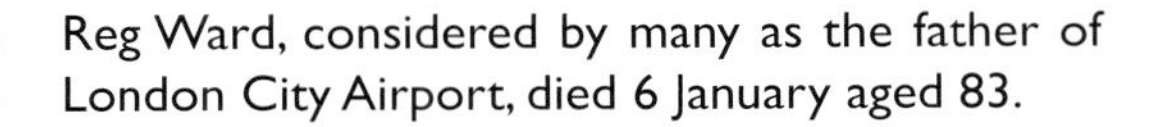
Reg Ward, considered by many as the father of London City Airport, died 6 January aged 83.

January: The airport welcomed the High Court decision following a Judicial Review which would allow for an upgrade of aircraft movements to 112,000 per year.

January: CityJet began new routes to Deauville, Florence and Pau; Skywork to Berne and Blue Islands to Jersey.

May: CityJet started summer routes to Toulon and Avignon.

June: BA began services to Faro and Malaga.

August: The DLR extension from Canning Town to Stratford and the Olympic Park was opened, and with it a link to London Overground. This added to the existing connection at Shadwell with the northbound Overground services to Whitechapel, Shoreditch and Dalston. Southbound the track goes to Surrey Quays with connections to the South London network as far as Gatwick.

November: The airport announced the retirement of Richard Gooding as Chief Executive, replaced by Declan Collier, previously Chief Executive of Dublin Airport Authority from 2005. Mr Gooding was retained on the airport board as Non-executive Director.

Aston Martin getaway for newly weds.

In Britain the wedding of Prince William and Catherine Middleton took place at Westminster Abbey on 29 April with an estimated worldwide audience of two billion people. A public holiday celebrated the day, which in conjunction with the May Bank Holiday, made a four-day weekend.

The event rather overshadowed the referendum which took place the following week. The Alternative Vote (AV) referendum concerned whether or not to replace the present 'first-past-the-post' system with the AV method. The proposal to introduce AV was rejected by the electorate. On a turnout of 42.2%, 68% voted 'No' and 32% voted 'Yes'.

The anti-austerity movement in the United Kingdom saw major demonstrations throughout 2011 including the London march which drew in a crowd of 500,000. Separate to these demonstrations were riots that occurred in England from 6 to 11 August. The unrest began when a police officer shot and killed 29-year-old Mark Duggan during an intelligence-led targeted vehicle stop procedure which was investigating gun crime within the black community. Thousands of people joined the riots across England and the resulting chaos generated looting, arson, and mass deployment of police and the death of five people. Over 200 people were injured.

In international news on 4 January Tunisian Mohamed Bouazizi died after setting himself on fire a month earlier, sparking anti-government protests in Tunisia and later other Arab nations including Libya, Egypt, Yemen, Syria and Iraq. These protests became known collectively as the Arab Spring. In Tunisia simmering public anger and sporadic violence intensified following Bouazizi's death, leading then-President Zine El Abidine Ben Ali to step down on 14 January, after 23 years in power. In Egypt the Government was overthrown and on 11 February President Hosni Mubarak resigned facing charges of killing unarmed activists. In Libya protests started a civil war between opposition forces and Muammar Gaddafi loyalists. The Government was overthrown and President Gaddafi killed by transition forces.

On 11 March an earthquake off the Pacific coast of Tohoku was the most powerful earthquake ever recorded to have hit Japan. Nearly 16,000 died, over 6,100 were injured and more than 228,000 people were either temporarily or permanently relocated. Around 4.4 million households in north-eastern Japan were left without electricity and 1.5 million without water. The World Bank's estimated economic cost of the earthquake was $235 billion, making it the costliest natural disaster in world history.

On 2 May United States President Barack Obama announced that Osama bin Laden, the founder and leader of the militant group al-Qaeda, had been killed in a US-led mission in Pakistan.

In sport, the England cricket team won The Ashes series 3–1 in Australia.

Famous people that died in 2011 included Muammar Gaddafi, Libyan President; Betty Ford, First Lady of the United States; Lucian Freud, painter; Amy Winehouse, singer songwriter; Elizabeth Taylor, actress; Sir Jimmy Savile, latterly disgraced television presenter; Steve Jobs, CEO of Apple and Pixar.

2012

Passenger total 3,016,664.

Passenger increase 0.8% on the previous year.
Number of flights 70,781, up 3.5%.

With the Olympics as the background Queen Elizabeth visited the airport, this time accompanied by Prince Philip. Hosted by new Airport Director Declan Collier, Her Majesty met with long serving employees, members of the local community, representatives of the owners, the Mayor of Newham and children from the Richard House Hospice, the airport's main charity. She unveiled a plaque commemorating her visit.

Figures published show that the airport supported 2,700 jobs, contributed £21 million in Air Passenger Duty, with £197 million spent by business people and tourists using the airport.

Manned by 'London Ambassadors' the airport hosted what was termed 'an information pod' throughout the Olympic and Paralympic Games period. The job of the team was not just to answer questions about the Olympics but encourage visitors to take in all that London offered.

March: CAA statistics showed London City Airport to be the most punctual airport in the United Kingdom.

Alitalia introduced the Embraer E190 to Milan and CityJet launched a new route to Brest with a Fokker 50.

April: British Airways began services to Aberdeen with a Embraer 170, and followed up in May with flights to the Balearics, Angers and Quimper, pure holiday routes.

June: British Airways introduced an all-year-round route to Palma and Ibiza.

Above: *The Queen fitted in LCY during a visit to East London during the Olympics, seen here with Declan Collier.*

Left: *Team GB swimming team arrives for the Olympics. Extra accommodation was provided by cruise ships.*

On a glorious Saturday night Great Britain and Northern Ireland won three Olympic Gold medals.

London, and in particular East London, was showcased to the world in 2012 when it played host to the Olympic and Paralympic Games. Key to the Games were former Olympic champion, Lord Coe, the Chairman of the Organising Committee, and Danny Boyle, who directed the opening ceremony – which famously included the 'Queen' jumping out of a helicopter with James Bond. The Games cost £9 billion with Transport for London (TfL) making numerous improvements to the infrastructure including the expansion of the London Overground's East London Line, upgrades to the Docklands Light Railway and the North London Line, and the introduction of a new 'Javelin' high-speed rail service.

TfL also built a £60 million cable car across the River Thames, called the Emirates Air Line, to link Olympic Games venues. It crosses the Thames between Greenwich Peninsula and the Royal Docks, carrying up to 2,500 passengers an hour, cutting journey times between the O2 arena and the ExCeL London exhibition centre and providing a crossing every 30 seconds.

It was Britain's most successful Olympics ever. Team GB won 65 medals at the Olympics, including 12 golds on 5 August (the so-called 'Super Saturday') and 120 medals at the Paralympics. During the Games, Michael Phelps became the most decorated Olympic athlete of all time, winning his 22nd medal. Women's boxing was included, thus the Games became the first at which every sport had female competitors.

It was also the year of Queen Elizabeth's Diamond Jubilee. Commemorative events included the Thames Diamond Jubilee Pageant on the River Thames (a maritime parade of 1,000 boats from around the Commonwealth) and a cavalcade to celebrate the Queen's visits to and tours of over 250 countries as well as her passion for horses.

Other British news included the launch of a police investigation into claims of sexual abuse by Jimmy Savile after ITV's programme documenting Savile's history. The television presenter had died the year before.

Relations with Islamist regimes were a key theme in the news – the European Union adopted an embargo against Iran in protest of its continued effort to enrich uranium. In response Iran suspended oil exports to Britain and France. Canada also cut diplomatic ties with Iran. On 11 September, the United States diplomatic mission in Benghazi was attacked by a heavily armed group of 125–150 Islamist gunmen killing four including the US Ambassador and injuring ten others.

Other international news included a ceasefire between Israel and the Palestinian terrorist group Hamas after the week-long escalation in hostilities in southern Israel and Gaza; the agreement of Eurozone finance ministers to its second bailout of the Greek government for €130 billion and the end of the Arab Spring protests which began the previous year.

Famous people that died included Neil Armstrong, astronaut; Vidal Sassoon, hairstylist and businessman; Larry Hagman, actor; Whitney Houston, singer and actress; and Sir Patrick Moore, astrologer and television presenter.

2013

Passenger total 3,390,264.

Passenger increase 12.4% on the previous year.
Number of flights 73,713, up 4.14%.

The new shop outlets and refreshment concerns on the first floor were completed.

British Airways celebrated its tenth anniversary at London City Airport with Willie Walsh, the former Chief Executive of British Airways, and by then heading up BA owner International Airlines Group (IAG), attending a celebration party held at the Docklands Museum in the West India Docks.

Which? magazine confirmed that London City Airport was the easiest London airport to reach by train. The DLR scored 81% in a customer survey with the Heathrow Express lagging behind, attaining a score of 70% and Gatwick Express tallying just 60%.

January: CityJet launched a new route to Nuremburg.

April: CityJet launched new routes to Dresden and Paderborn and Alitalia launched a new route to Rome.

July: British Airways launched a new route to Granada.

July: City Airport Development Programme (CADP) planning application submitted to Newham Council.

British Airways Cityflyer launched service to Düsseldorf.

Lady Thatcher passed away.

On the 8 April Lady (Margaret) Thatcher, Britain's first female Prime Minister, aged 87, passed away following a stroke. She received a ceremonial funeral, including full military honours, with a church service at St Paul's Cathedral. It was attended by Queen Elizabeth, Prince Philip, all four of the living UK Prime Ministers, the Prime Ministers of Canada and South Africa, Hillary Clinton, other foreign dignitaries, and all United Kingdom Government Ministers.

The following month on 22 May two men carrying knives and a meat cleaver killed a serving off-duty British soldier, Drummer Lee Rigby, in a street in Woolwich. His murderers were subsequently shot and wounded before being apprehended by police. The Government treated the killing as a terrorist incident and the two men were sentenced to life imprisonment.

Other British news included the birth of Prince George of Cambridge – who is third in line to the throne; the Scottish Government announced that the loss-making Prestwick Airport in Glasgow was to be taken into public ownership. Same sex marriage became legal in England and Wales.

The death of Nelson Mandela, first President of South Africa, on 5 December was the biggest news story. The anti-apartheid icon, aged 95, had been receiving intensive medical care at home for a lung infection after spending three months in hospital. His funeral took place ten days later following more than a week of national mourning. At least 80 foreign heads of state and government travelled to South Africa to attend memorial events including American President Barack Obama, three former Presidents of the United States, British Prime Minister David Cameron and Prince Charles, who represented the Queen.

In international news Pope Benedict XVI unexpectedly announced his resignation on grounds of poor health, making him the first pope to do so in nearly 600 years. Cardinal Jorge Mario Bergoglio from Argentina was subsequently elected as Pope Francis.

Following a military coup in Egypt, two anti-coup camps were raided by the security forces leaving 2,600 dead. The raids were described by Human Rights Watch as 'one of the world's largest killings of demonstrators in a single day in recent history'. In Russia a meteor exploded over the city of Chelyabinsk, injuring over 1,400 people and damaging over 4,300 buildings. It was the most powerful meteor to strike earth's atmosphere in over a century. The European Union finally agreed to a €10 billion economic bailout for Cyprus. Croatia became the 28th member of the European Union.

The year 2013 will also be remembered for the first British men's single win at Wimbledon since Fred Perry in 1936 when Andy Murray beat Novak Djokovic in straight sets at Wimbledon. Murray also won *BBC Sports Personality of the Year*. The Rugby World Cup took place in England and Australia won beating New Zealand 34–2 in the final to lift the Rugby League World Cup for the tenth time.

Others who died included Seamus Heaney, Irish Nobel poet; Doris Lessing, British Nobel writer; Michael Winner, film director and restaurant critic; Ronnie Biggs, British criminal.

2014

Passenger total 3,647,824.

Passenger increase up 12.4% on the previous year.
Number of flights 73,713, up 4.14%.

London City Airport was listed as a top global airport with regard to the visual approach alongside Nice Côte d'Azur, Rio and Gibraltar, in a travel poll conducted by PrivateFly, the executive aviation specialist.

The airport was named 'Airport of the Year' in its category at the 2014 Air Transport News Awards. London City picked up the accolade for the best airport with under ten million passengers per year at a ceremony in Istanbul. London City Airport also won the 'World's Best Airport' award in the category for airports serving under five million passengers at the 2014 World Airport Awards at the Passenger Terminal Expo in Barcelona.

Making a return to the airport was Flybe which signed a five-year agreement and launched domestic and international operations from 27 October to Belfast, Dublin, Edinburgh, Exeter and Inverness, using 78-seat Bombardier Q400 turboprops in a 2+2 seat layout.

Air France sold CityJet/VLM to Intro Aviation of Germany who themselves disposed of the Dutch part of the package to its management. (VLM went into receivership in 2016 but by mid-2017 the assets and name had been resurrected by SHS Aviation, a Slovakian operator backed by Dutch interests.)

Aurigny launched a London City to Guernsey service, which was to last until the end of the summer season 2017.

The airport introduced an aviation industry training and recruitment programme developed in conjunction with Newham Council's employment service Workplace. A group of 12 recruits were chosen for the six-month Ramp Academy scheme, which offered employment opportunities in Newham.

London Airport led the way in installing a self-service security arrangement, since copied by many airports.

The first Invictus Games was held in London with Prince Harry very much the centre piece.

It was a quiet year in terms of British news. The Scottish referendum took place in September with 55.3% of the population voting to stay as part of the United Kingdom (with a voter turnout of 84.5%). Following the referendum Nicola Sturgeon succeeded Alex Hammond as the leader of the SNP. It was also the year that Andy Coulson, the former managing editor of *News of the World*, along with some of his other colleagues, were jailed as part of the phone hacking scandal; and entertainer Rolf Harris was found guilty of 12 counts of indecent assault between 1968 and 1986.

The Ukrainian revolution took place early in the year, when a series of violent protests in the capital, Kiev, culminated in the ousting of Ukrainian President, Viktor Yanukovych. As the unrest spread Russian troops invaded the Crimea and a new pro-Russian Prime Minister was installed. Russia was then suspended from G8 and international sanctions were introduced.

There were two disturbing air disasters in 2014 – both on Malaysian Airlines. In March Flight MH370, a Boeing 777 airliner en route to Beijing from Kuala Lumpur, disappeared over the Gulf of Thailand with 239 people on board. The cause of its disappearance is still unknown. In July Flight MH17, a scheduled passenger flight from Amsterdam to Kuala Lumpur, was shot down while flying over eastern Ukraine, killing all 283 passengers and 15 crew on board. The investigation into the crash concluded that the airliner was downed by a Buk surface-to-air missile launched from pro-Russian separatist-controlled territory in Ukraine.

In the Middle East three Israeli teenagers were kidnapped and in response Israel launched Operation Protective Edge against the Hamas-controlled Gaza Strip. In seven weeks of fighting 2,100 Palestinians and 71 Israelis were killed. In Syria almost 200,000 people lost their lives in the escalating conflict between forces loyal to President Bashar al-Assad.

The Ebola virus which broke out this year in West Africa was first reported and rapidly became the deadliest occurrence of the disease since its discovery in 1976. More than 6,500 people were reported to have died from the disease.

It was a busy year for sport with the Winter Olympics, the World Cup, the Commonwealth Games, and a new competition the Invictus Games. The Winter Olympic Games took place in Sochi, Russia, with Team GB winning one gold, one silver and two bronze – their most successful Winter Games since Innsbruck in 1984. In the World Cup in Brazil, England were eliminated in the first round and Germany went on to win the Cup. The Commonwealth Games took place in Glasgow and England topped the medals table winning 58 golds. The first Invictus Games were held in London at the Queen Elizabeth Olympic Park. The Games are an international Paralympic style multi-sport event, created by Prince Harry, for injured armed services personnel. The Games were deemed to be a great success.

South African Paralympian Oscar Pistorius was sentenced to five years in jail for killing his girlfriend Reeva Steenkamp. Ms Steenkamp was in Pistorius' bathroom when she was shot – he claimed that he thought she was an intruder.

Famous people who died included Tony Benn, politician; Ariel Sharon, Israeli Prime Minister; Shirley Temple, actress; Bob Hoskins, actor; Rik Mayall, comedian; Robin Williams, comedian and actor, Lauren Bacall, actress; Lord (Richard) Attenborough, actor and film director and Joan Rivers, comedian.

2015

Passenger total 4,319,521.

Passenger increase 4.5% on the previous year.
Number of flights 84,753, up 11%.

The Embraer Phenom 300 began flight operations from the Executive Jet Centre from February with NetJets Europe. It can carry up to seven occupants and has a flying range of 1,971 nautical miles. It is the most successful in the category of 'light business jets'.

Work began to expand the Western Pier, which houses 70% of the departure gates. The change was as dramatic as the roofing over of the check-in area a decade earlier. The finished pier created a bright, open-plan space with modern seating, workspaces, quiet areas and charging points. Waiting for an aircraft one could sit by a window and watch the view with one eye on the departure board. The boarding gate would only be steps away. The area was designed to take pressure off the existing waiting zone with 600 additional seats, plus space for new retail and food and beverage units.

June saw the one millionth Luxair passenger pass through, a milestone for the airline that has been with London City Airport since 2003. Ten years after their launch they increased their number of flights to Luxembourg City (the nation's capital) to five a day. In 2014 that went up to six and then in April 2015 it reached seven a day.

NetJets Europe Phenom 300 makes its first arrival at LCY.

Jeremy Corbyn, who had never held a senior Labour post before, becomes leader of the Labour Party.

This was election year in Britain and a television debate between the three Party leaders took place for the first time. The Conservative Party won an outright majority securing David Cameron's second term in office; the SNP gained almost total power in Scotland (56 out of 59 seats), the Labour Party lost 26 seats and the Liberal Democrats were almost wiped out with just eight of their previous 57 remaining. Ed Miliband, Nick Clegg and Nigel Farage, the three respective leaders of Labour, Liberal Democrats and UKIP, all announced their resignations in the wake of their election defeats. Ed Miliband was swapped controversially with the left-wing politician Jeremy Corbyn, who had never held a senior Labour post before; Nick Clegg was replaced with Tim Farron and Nigel Farage subsequently became the acting leader of UKIP until November 2016.

In other news the second child of the Duke and Duchess of Cambridge, Princess Charlotte Elizabeth Diana, was born on 2 May; Queen Elizabeth II became Britain's longest-reigning monarch on 9 September at 17:30 – surpassing her great-grandmother Queen Victoria. Jeremy Clarkson, the *Top Gear* presenter, was fired by the BBC following an incident when the presenter verbally and physically abused the programme's producer Oisin Tymon; England became the last United Kingdom country to introduce a 5p charge for plastic carrier bags at stores and supermarkets; and the Eurotunnel migrant crisis worsened as it was reported that 2,000 illegal migrants tried to enter the Channel Tunnel terminal at Calais in an attempt to reach the United Kingdom in one night.

In international news, on 7 January in Paris two gunmen belonging to al-Qaeda's Yemen branch, shot and killed 12 people and injured 11 others at the offices of French satirical magazine *Charlie Hebdo*. Three other terrorist attacks also took place in the Île-de-France region over the next two days, including at a kosher supermarket, killing a further five people and injuring 11. The attacks further prompted an anti-terrorism demonstration in Paris attended by over a million people and more than 40 world leaders. The phrase 'Je suis Charlie' became a common slogan of support at the rallies and in social media.

In June a mass shooting occurred at a tourist resort near Sousse in Tunisia. A gunman, Seifeddine Rezgui, attacked a hotel killing 38 people, 30 of whom were British. The Tunisian Government later acknowledged fault for a slow police response to the attack.

In business news automaker Volkswagen was found to have been involved in worldwide rigging of diesel emissions tests, affecting an estimated 11 million vehicles globally. Volkswagen's stock price fell in value by a third in the days immediately after the news and the cars affected were recalled to be refitted.

In sport FIFA President Sepp Blatter announced his intention to resign amidst an FBI-led corruption investigation, surrounding 14 people within the organisation. Great Britain's Chris Froome won the 2015 Tour de France – the third win in four years by a British rider – and tennis player Andy Murray helped lead Great Britain to the Davis Cup title for the first time in 79 years.

Famous people that died included Lord (Leon) Britton and Charles Kennedy, politicians; Sir Martin Gilbert, historian; Cilla Black, singer and presenter; Oliver Sacks, neurologist; Sir Nicholas Winton, humanitarian; King Abdullah of Saudi Arabia, Jackie Collins, author and Natalie Cole, singer.

2016

Passenger total 4,538,735.

Passenger increase 5% on the previous year.
Number of flights 85,169, a factor increase as the aircraft load factor improved.

This was the year the airport 'came of age' and 30 years since the Prince of Wales laid the foundation stone for the terminal. On 11 July, 18,641 travellers passed through the airport, a record number to date.

Chancellor of the Exchequer Philip Hammond, a former Transport Secretary, was at the airport in July to formally confirm approval for a new £350 million expansion programme. Earlier, in February, the sale of the airport was announced by Global Infrastructure Partners (75%) and Oaktree Capital Management (25%) to a consortium comprising Alberta Investment Management Corporation, OMERS, the Ontario Teachers' Pension Plan and Wren House for a reported £2.3 billion.

Another piece of news was the result of *The Independent's* annual survey of transport links to the United Kingdom's leading airports, placing London City first! The survey rates airports on the off-peak frequency, journey time and cost of the main link to the city they serve.

Founder Pat Byrne and private equity backers repurchased Irish regional airline CityJet from German owner Intro Aviation for an undisclosed sum.

The Danish airline SUN-AIR, a franchise partner of British Airways for the last 20 years, commenced a ten times weekly Bremen service on 31 October with a 32-seat Dornier 328 regional aircraft offering a meal and snacks, ice cream dessert and daily newspapers.

British Airways itself strengthened its German network with flights to Berlin and Hamburg, and added a further Embraer E190 bringing the fleet strength up to 20 aircraft. A service to Alicante was also introduced, the seventh to Spain taking the 2016 total up to 33 destinations.

The City Airport Development Programme (CADP) was announced which included plans for seven new aircraft stands, a parallel taxiway and passenger terminal extension, enabling 6.5 million passengers to use the airport by 2025.

Flybe reintroduced services to Cardiff initially as 'rescue flights', due to the closure of the Severn Tunnel. These continued after the tunnel reopened.

Now one of Newham's largest employers, the airport distributed a pledge to over 30,000 households in the borough, promising increased hiring, broader community and schools outreach and local charity fundraising. A ComRes survey showed that 77% of East London business decision-makers supported London City Airport's expansion plans.

Declan Collier welcomes Chancellor of the Exchequer Philip Hammond (centre) and the then Transport Minister Tariq Ahmad (right).

Remodelled West Pier reopened giving a much brighter welcome to the departure gates.

(Sir) Terry Wogan died suddenly, the doyen of TV presenters.

Britain was gripped by Brexit in 2016 – the British referendum to decide whether Britain should stay in the European Union. However just before the election, on 16 June, Labour MP Jo Cox was shot and stabbed to death by Thomas Mair, a white supremacist, as she prepared to hold a meeting with constituents in Birstall, West Yorkshire. The murder brought sobriety to the Brexit campaigns.

On 23 June people in Britain voted to leave the European Union by a small margin – 52.9% to 48.1% on a national turnout of 72%. London's stock market plunged more than 8% in the wake of the result, with the pound falling to its lowest level against the dollar since 1985. Prime Minister David Cameron who had campaigned to remain, immediately resigned following the result and was succeeded by Theresa May on 13 July. The Labour Party faced a leadership challenge after the result but Jeremy Corbyn, its hard left leader, won and remained as party leader.

Other British news included the government approval for a third runway at Heathrow Airport with Zac Goldsmith MP for Richmond Park resigning in protest and Sir Philip Green's British Home Stores (BHS) went into administration – making 11,000 people redundant and leaving a gaping hole of £571 million in pension liabilities.

In the United States, as with Brexit, the electorate voted differently to pollsters expectations. After a bitter presidential election campaign, Republican Donald Trump, a businessman and former reality television star, won the American election against a previous Secretary of State and First Lady Democrat Hillary Clinton. Trump won the 304 electoral votes whilst Clinton gained 227 but Clinton won the popular vote by nearly three million. Following the announcement of Donald Trump's election, large protests broke out across the United States with some continuing for several days.

In other international news, on 22 March three coordinated bombings in Brussels, Belgium killed at least 32 and injured at least 250. The Islamic State of Iraq and the Levant claimed responsibility for the attacks – two of the bombs were at Brussels Airport in Zaventem, and one at Maalbeek metro station in central Brussels. Another terrorist attack also took place on 19 December when a truck was driven into the Christmas market next to the Kaiser Wilhelm Memorial Church at Breitscheidplatz in Berlin, which left 12 people dead and 56 others injured.

Summer was a season of British sporting triumphs. Andy Murray won Wimbledon, underdogs Leicester City won the premiership, and Team GB delivered their best medal tally in years at the Rio 2016 Olympic Games.

Many celebrity icons passed away in 2016. These included David Bowie, musician, Sir 'Terry' Wogan, broadcaster; Sir George Martin, 'the fifth Beatle'; Prince, singer; Leonard Cohen, singer and poet; George Michael, singer and Muhammad Ali, boxer. Political figures who died included Nancy Reagan, First Lady of the United States and actress, Elie Wiesel, author; Shimon Peres, President and Prime Minister of Israel, Fidel Castro, Prime Minister of Cuba; as well as Jo Cox, the first sitting Member of Parliament to be murdered.

2017

Having been involved in the airport since its inauguration by Queen Elizabeth in 1987, Roy Griffins stepped down as Chairman, being replaced by Sir Terry Morgan, Chairman of Crossrail (Elizabeth Line).

In March Bombardier paid a surprise visit to London City Airport with the brand new Bombardier CS100, carrying out a series of test flights. It finally departed non-stop to New York, arriving just over seven hours later. Is it a prelude to future services?

At the completion of the winter season Air France, the longest continuous operator, ceased their flights to Paris, which had been flown in partnership with CityJet.

The west wing of the airport revealed a much brighter access to the stands, also comprising a new series of retail units including Brick Lane Brews offering a selection of East London's best artisan products to customers.

KLM Royal Dutch Airlines returned to the airport after an absence of almost eight years, partnering CityJet on flights to Amsterdam.

Declan Collier resigned as London City Airport Chief Executive Officer after five years in charge and overseeing a 50% rise in passenger numbers.

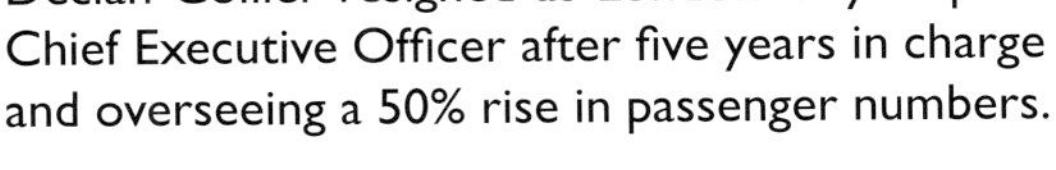
Left: *Making a return to London City was KLM with up to eight Embraer services daily to Amsterdam.*

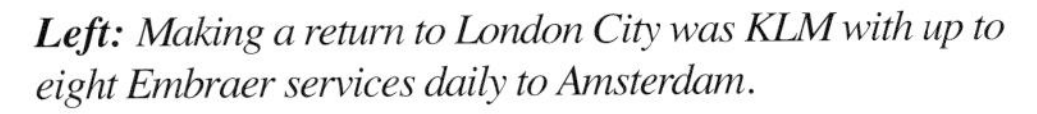
Below: *Non-stop to New York for the first time in March. Bombardier CS100.*

Chapter Ten
The aircraft

British Aerospace BAe 146 and Avro RJ

David Dorman was British Aerospace Commercial Aircraft Division (BAe) Director Public Relations and Marketing 1985–92. Here he takes up the story of Britain's most successful jet airliner – the four-engined BAe 146 and its successor – the Avro RJ. In total 394 were built of which around 220 were in service in the middle of 2017. The RJX (first flight May 2001) was the final development of the aircraft before BAE Systems terminated the project in November 2001.

Britain's finest airliner

Whilst it is true that London City Airport could not have happened without the Dash 7, it undoubtedly would not be where it is today without the BAe/Avro RJ. Strange to say that both owe their heritage to Sir Geoffrey de Havilland, founder of the company that bore his name, and based at Hatfield, North London. The BAe 146 started life at that plant. The DHC Dash 7 was the last in a line of specialised short take-off aircraft produced by the Canadian de Havilland offspring.

In August 1973, Hawker Siddeley Aviation (which had acquired de Havilland), launched a new 70-seat regional jet airliner project. Following the DH numbering system this was the HS 146. It was designed to fill the gap between turboprop-powered airliners like the HS 748 and the Fokker F 27 and small jet airliners such as the BAC One-Eleven and Boeing 737. The chosen configuration had a high wing and a T-tail to give good short-field performance, while the aircraft was to be powered by four 6500 lb thrust Avco Lycoming ALF 502H turbofan engines.

The programme was initially launched with backing from the UK Government, which agreed to contribute 50% of the development costs in return for a share of the revenues from each aircraft sold. In October 1974, however, all work on the project was halted as a result of the world economic downturn resulting from the 1973 oil crisis.

But low-key development proceeded and in 1978 British Aerospace (the newly nationalised aerospace company formed from Hawker Siddeley, British Aircraft Corporation and Scottish Aviation) relaunched the project as the BAe 146 – seen as a key element of its plan to revitalise the UK civil aircraft manufacturing business. British Aerospace marketed the aircraft as a quiet, low-consumption turbofan aircraft, which would be effective at replacing the previous generation of turboprop-powered feeder aircraft.

The first of three development aircraft flew in 1981 and initial flight results showed better-than-predicted take-off and climb performance. The BAe 146 received a Certificate of Airworthiness on 8 February 1983. Upon its launch into service later that year with Dan-Air of the UK and Air Wisconsin of the USA, it was hailed as being 'the world's quietest jetliner'.

And on to London City

But the behind the scenes story of how the BAe 146 overcame hurdles to become the first jet airliner to operate from London City and to dominate the market there for over 20 years is worth telling.

British Aerospace (now BAE Systems Regional Aircraft) first started quietly working on the possibility of its BAe 146 being able to operate from the planned new airport as early as 1985 – only two years after the aircraft had first entered service and one year before construction of the airport started in 1986.

The BAe 146 with its high wing, four-engine design, similar to the Dash 7, had sparkling airfield performance. Unlike the Dash 7 which was a dedicated STOL (short take-off and landing) aircraft, the BAe 146 would not be able to function realistically from the planned declared runway length of 762m, but could operate, for demonstration purposes, from the full runway length of 1030m.

The advantages of the BAe 146 were obvious. It offered twice the speed, twice the range, a much bigger payload, leading to much better revenue and profit potential for operators and a greatly increased range of destinations. For the passenger it offered the benefits of the smoother jet experience. For the local community, the 'whisperjet' – as it had become known – was a good neighbour with a very low noise profile.

Air brakes in use on the BAe 146.

Moreover, it had just started in production (unlike the Dash 7 which was out of production) and was beginning to attract significant orders, notably from key airlines in the USA which were using the aircraft to operate from very noise sensitive airports in California.

In 1986–87 British Aerospace's engineering and sales teams at Hatfield worked up the case for the BAe 146 to operate from a developed London City Airport. The company recognised that if a way could be found to operate the quadjet from such a difficult airport as LCY then this could lead to strong worldwide interest and possible further sales.

Bill Charnock was Managing Director LCY 1988–96. He says about the BAe 146:

'Whilst the aircraft itself was the key element in making it possible at the time for the airport to fulfil its potential, and the involvement and co-operation of British Aerospace at every level with the airport management could not have been better, it is equally true that the airport's subsequent success could not have been achieved without a number of other critically important elements coming into place.'

Another vital factor was the need for a credible launch operator for the aircraft. Bill Charnock describes how Moritz Suter, the visionary founder and Chief Executive of Swiss airline Crossair visited the airport, went on his knees and said: 'I want to operate here.' Crossair, which had taken delivery of three BAe 146s in 1990, subsequently pioneered the first London City Airport jet services in 1992.

BAe found itself closely involved in discussions with the London Docklands Development Corporation (LDDC), and also with Olympia & York, the Canadian developers of Canary Wharf. Both were hugely supportive of the airport and saw the potential for the proposed BAe 146 operations.

But much work had to be done before the aircraft would be allowed to operate from London City Airport.

A demonstration of the aircraft, alongside the Dash 7, took place on Saturday 24 July 1988 as the first stage in the exercises of public education and consultation prior to the submission of a formal planning application to develop the airport for use by the BAe 146. Two BAe 146s were used – one in the colours of Loganair, the Scottish airline – which was put on static display to allow members of the public

Avro twins – the BAe quad jet proved popular for both British Airways and Air France.

to get a closer view. Of note was the fact that the BAe 146 whilst wider than the Dash 7 had in fact a smaller wingspan.

A second aircraft, in BAe house colours, ballasted inside to represent full operational weights, was used to fly a number of take-offs, landings and fly-bys at 500 feet and 2,000 feet – manoeuvres replicated exactly by the Dash 7. Comprehensive noise measurements were taken. The BAe 146 showed that it could approach the short runway down a 5.5-degree slope and could climb out with ample clearance over existing tower buildings and cranes.

The LCY management team had leafleted every household in the district explaining what was going on and thousands of people came to watch. A carnival atmosphere was created with jazz bands, refreshments and a children's play area. There were some protesters outside the main terminal building, but when they realised that they had not heard the 'whisperjets' land, they were invited inside to join the party.

The local reaction, media comment and subsequent opinion polls showed overwhelming support for the airport development.

Behind the scenes work

However it was over a year before a new planning application was lodged in September 1989 and the subsequent Public Inquiry took place between early July and the end of 1990. The application asked for the runway length to be increased to 1199m (a Code 2 runway) to accommodate semi-STOL aircraft like the BAe 146 (the only jet capable of operating at the airport at the time) and more modern turboprops such as the Fokker 50, Dash 8-100/300, ATR-42, Saab 340 and Dornier 328.

In addition, much work went on behind the scenes by airport management working closely with local enterprises and BAe to ensure that the plethora of tall buildings either built or planned in the vicinity of the airport would not impede safe and economic aircraft operations.

To the east of the airport the proposed East London River Crossing (ELRC) bridge was a potential concern. To the west the main Canary Wharf Tower and secondary towers also posed problems.

The first priority was to reconcile the Canary Wharf main tower and demonstrate that it lay beneath two clearance surfaces – the Aerodrome and Ground Aids (AGA) surface and the ILS OAS (Instrument Landing System Obstacle Assessment Surface). Penetration of the ILS OAS by the tower would make the tower an accountable obstacle which would raise decision heights and bring about an unacceptably high non-availability; failure to comply with the AGA surface would prevent the granting of an aerodrome licence.

The Canary Wharf tower had been granted planning consent for a height of 834 feet and it was thought that the BAe 146 would be able to fly a 5-degree glide slope. However, at the planned tower height both the AGA and ILS OAS were intercepted by the building.

This situation was resolved in three ways. Firstly, flight tests showed the BAe 146 could achieve a steeper 5.5-degree glide path; secondly Olympia & York, agreed to reduce the height of the main tower to 784 feet; and thirdly the CAA agreed to some changes in glide path angle and other technical changes resulting in compatibility being achieved between the tower and the proposed developed airport. The calculation, negotiation and persuasion to achieve that resolution took considerable time and effort.

To the east of the airport, where most approaches occur, the proposed ELRC design with its cable stay structure and high towers would have rendered the airport development impossible to achieve. A report submitted to the inspector at the ELRC Public Inquiry pointed out the implications for the airport and offered a different design as a box girder shallow arch bridge.

Eventually the Inspector, followed by the Secretary of State, agreed that a revised bridge design was required and it was this revised design that was considered at the concurrent ELRC/ London City Airport Public Inquiry in 1990 and thereafter approved.

The airport's approach conditions had been defined largely in terms of the four-engined BAe 146; take-off for the aircraft was not an issue given that the engine-out case for a quadjet is much superior to that of a twin.

In terms of noise, the strict regime around the airport was easily complied with by the 'whisperjet' BAe 146 and the aircraft remains compliant.

Consent to extend the runway was given in September 1991 and this led to a relatively small amount of construction work. The airport in its revised form was licensed by the CAA before Christmas 1991.

Flying the BAe 146/Avro RJ into LCY

To enable the BAe 146 to operate the steep 5.5-degree approach British Aerospace had to design a 'steep approach mod' and revised operational procedures for the aircraft. Basically this adds the steep approach appendix to the Aircraft Flight Manual and desensitises some Ground Proximity Warning System (GPWS) modes so the crew does not get a call-out at the higher rates of descent. Also to achieve the 5.5-degree approach an abuse case of 7.5 degrees had to be demonstrated.

To achieve certification BAe test pilots had to fly the steep approach and demonstrate an actual engine failure at decision height to land and similar to go around. Once those test schedules had been completed the Civil Aviation Authority (CAA) and European Aviation Safety Agency (EASA) checked the data and they also did some approaches at London City Airport to complete the certification.

Speed control for any aircraft flying into the airport is vital. Because the approach is steeper than usual it is difficult to lose speed and so aircraft need to be close to approach speed as they reach the glide path. With the quadjet it gets to the glideslope with 33-degree of flap and close to VREF (reference landing approach speed) +5 knots.

On glideslope interception, the airbrake is deployed (on a normal approach this does not happen until around 100 feet above the runway).

Having got to the threshold, the steep approach requires a greater attitude change to achieve the landing attitude, and this greater flare can lead to the possibility of a tail strike if allowed to go too far. To avoid this, BAe recommended that the non-handling pilot gives a call if the pitch attitude exceeds a predetermined value (which, of course, differs for all three aircraft lengths). All BAe146/ Avro RJs have reduced allowable tailwind limits for LCY.

BAe 146/Avro RJ training for LCY normally consists of one simulator session covering normal and emergency operations (such as engine failure on take-off, brake failure on landing). This would be followed up by several visits with a training captain. LCY is captain only landing – the flight officers do take-offs and go-arounds. There will be some recurrent simulator checking and some annual ground school refreshers.

An international lineup of BAe 146 and Avro RJ.

Jet services start

In February 1992 the BAe 146 (Series 100 and 200) were cleared to operate from LCY and after the newly extended runway at the airport was opened in March, Crossair launched the first BAe 146 flights to and from Zurich. Certification for the Series 300 followed in November 1994 and at that time three airlines were operating the BAe 146 into LCY – Business Air with the Series 200 (operating the Frankfurt route on behalf of Lufthansa), Virgin Atlantic (operated by CityJet) and Crossair.

Although British Aerospace had long been courting European airlines to sell the virtues of the quadjet together with operations from LCY some of the early companies that acquired the jet did not have big pockets, or the traffic was slow to materialise and some services did not last long. Gradually, however, some really credible operators selected the aircraft and the use of the BAe 146 – and by now the Avro RJ which was also cleared for operation – began to accelerate.

A measure of the success enjoyed is that by September 1998 eight out of 10 airlines operating at LCY were using BAe 146/Avro RJs – including many operating for flag carriers, such as Air France (CityJet), Alitalia (Azzurair), KLM (KLM uk), Lufthansa Cityline, Sabena (DAT), and Swissair (Crossair). In addition CityJet and Malmö Aviation operated in their own right. Nearly 70% of all scheduled movements at LCY were flown by the BAe jets.

During the early 2000s, more and more airlines started flying with the British jet, although some of the previous operators fell by the wayside over time. Probably the busiest time for quadjet operations was in the 2007–08 period. In April 2007 there were seven airlines flying the aircraft from LCY and the list of cities served was a roll call of European capitals and other prominent centres. Airlines flying the type included Air One of Italy (operated by Transwede), Air France/CityJet, British Airways Cityflyer, SAS, Lufthansa Cityline, SWISS and, for a short period, VLM of Belgium (operated by Flightline of the UK).

The following year, according to a study of the Official Airline Guide carried out by BAe, the BAe 146/Avro RJ accounted for 96% of all LCY scheduled jet traffic. In terms of overall scheduled traffic including turboprops, the jet was responsible for 54% of all scheduled daily departures and 70% of all weekly seats. In fact, 2008 was the peak year for BAe 146/Avro RJ operations at LCY.

But newer regional jets were on the horizon and when BA Cityflyer announced it was to re-equip its Avro RJ100 fleet with Embraer E-170/195 jets, which it started doing in 2009, then inevitably the dominance of the quadjet began to fade. Lufthansa Cityline – after 18 years of Avro RJ85 operations – also moved out of the type and SWISS announced they were going to re-equip with the Bombardier C Series. It was only in 2011 that scheduled movements from the Embraer E-Jets surpassed that of the BAe 146/ Avro RJ – a trend that has continued.

In early 2017 – 25 years after the Crossair BAe 146-200 had started the first jet operations from LCY – the BAe 146/Avro RJ still accounted for between 20–30% of all scheduled flights from the airport. SWISS ceased operations with the RJ100 from LCY in March 2017, replacing the aircraft with leased E-Jets from Helvetic until the C Series received its LCY certification which it was undergoing that same month.

Ireland's CityJet still operated the RJ85 from LCY in Spring 2017 on flights to Dublin, Amsterdam, Florence and Rotterdam, plus seasonal flights to Avignon and Toulon. CityJet's replacement for the RJ85 fleet is the Sukhoi SSJ-100 Superjet but CityJet is not pushing certification and say that the Avros will be flying between London and Dublin until at least 2020.

All told, nearly 20 airlines have flown the BAe 146/Avro RJ on scheduled services at differing times during the 25 years that the quadjet reigned supreme at LCY. In addition the BAe 146s of the Royal Air Force's No 32 (The Royal) Squadron have operated there as well as quadjets of ad-hoc ACMI (aircraft, crew, maintenance and insurance) operators flying on behalf of some of the regular airlines.

There is no doubt that the BAe 146/Avro RJ was pivotal in transforming the fortunes of the airport, but even as it parts company with LCY, the aircraft are finding new homes and roles overseas.

Some of the SWISS RJ100s that once operated to LCY are now to be found flying scheduled services in southern Chile and high into the Andes to serve mining stations. Others are starting new services from the British Virgin Islands in the Caribbean.

Some BA Cityflyer RJ100s are to be found operating in the fearsome heat of Western Australia, and by contrast in the ice wastes off remote northern Canada.

Many of the Lufthansa Cityline RJ85s are now flying in the demanding aerial firefighting role in North America, along with two of the original CityJet BAe 146-200s that were built in the late 1980s – a great testimony to the strength and durability of the aircraft. And closer to home, the two Air Jet BAe 146-200QCs that flew high-class services from LCY to Paris for a while are now to be found at RAF Northolt, operating as combined passenger and freight aircraft for the military.

These aircraft along with the ATP, BAe 748 and Jetstream turboprop – a total of 500 aircraft – are supported 24/7 by BAE Systems Regional Aircraft at Prestwick, Scotland. Some of the services offered are spares, engineering expertise, continued airworthiness, flight operations support, modification/upgrades, repairs and technical publications.

Brazil – Aviation and Embraer

Brazil can rightly say it was one of the pioneer nations when it comes to aviation. Alberto Santos-Dumont (1873–1932), usually referred to as simply Santos-Dumont, was a Brazilian innovator/inventor, one of the very few people to have contributed significantly to the development of both lighter-than-air and heavier-than-air aircraft.

The son of a wealthy farmer, engineer and inventor Henrique Dumont, known for a time as the 'Coffee King of Brazil', Santos-Dumont was educated in Paris. In his early career he designed, built and flew hot air balloons and dirigibles, culminating in winning the Deutsch de la Meurthe prize on 19 October 1901 for a flight that circled the Eiffel Tower. This made him world famous. He then turned to heavier-than-air machines, and on 23 October 1906 his model 14-bis made the first powered heavier-than-air flight in Europe to be certified by the Aéro-Club de France and the

Fédération Aéronautique Internationale. It was a project we might call today 'design – build – fly'.

In 1904, after Santos-Dumont complained to his friend Louis Cartier about the difficulty of checking his pocket watch during flight, Cartier created his first men's wristwatch, thus allowing Santos-Dumont to check his flight performance while keeping both hands on the controls.

Today, Cartier still markets a line of Santos-Dumont watches and sunglasses.

On 12 November 1906 he set the first world record recognized by the Fédération Aéronautique Internationale, by flying 220m (722ft) in 21.5 seconds in his own aircraft. Just as a comparison Usain Bolt would have kept up with him, the world record for 200m being 19.19 seconds.

By 1910 it was all over. Santos-Dumont gave up aviation and with increasing mental health problems he faded away, eventually committing suicide in Brazil. He was given a state funeral and is today considered the father of Brazilian aviation. You will not go far in Brazil without seeing something named after Santos-Dumont.

Jump forward to 1969.

In the immediate post World War II period Brazil relied for the most part on surplus military aircraft and aeroplanes developed by the major aircraft manufacturers. At General Aviation level Beech, Cessna and Piper reigned supreme. With vast distances between the main conurbations it was a country crying out for a domestic aviation industry.

Seeking to develop a domestic aircraft industry, the Brazilian Government made several investments during the 1940s and 1950s without much success. In 1969 Empresa Brasileira de Aeronáutica (Embraer) was created as a State-owned corporation. Home was to be São José dos Campos, already the site of The Instituto Tecnológico de Aeronáutica (ITA) a public institution for higher education and advanced research with emphasis in aerospace science and technology. ITA is rated as one of the top and most prestigious engineering schools in Brazil. In a true multi-national country Brazil was able to recruit specialists from all over the world, including Japan. São José is about 50 miles, or a one hour drive north from São Paulo International Airport.

Under the direction of Brazil's first President, the dynamic Ozires Silva, an engineer and government appointee, the company initially produced the EMB 110 Bandeirante unveiling it to the world at the Paris Air Show in 1971.

Straight away it was a big success, a simple unpressurised 21-seat turboprop commuter aircraft competing with the more basic de Havilland Twin Otter, and the Dornier 228. When production ceased in 1990 some 500 had been built.

Embraer Legacy 500 at the LCY Private Jet Centre.

In 1983 Embraer organised the first ever British press group to Brazil. The author can be seen in the centre.

The Bandeirante was succeeded by the EMB 121 Xingu in 1977, with the engines and wings of the Bandeirante and an all new pressurised cabin. With room for eight passengers maximum it could not compete with the high volume production of the then current US aircraft with similar capacity and performance. Only 106 were built.

Next up was a 30-seat regional fully pressurised aircraft called the EMB 120 Brasilia selling 354 around the world, the aircraft finding much favour with the military. It was built in a 15-year period from 1985 onwards.

A mention must be given at this point to the EMB 312 turboprop two-seat basic military trainer. Now due for retirement, and assembled by Shorts at Belfast, the Tucano has been in RAF service since 1989. A total of 664 units were produced (504 by Embraer and 160 by Short Brothers), flying in 16 air forces over five continents.

The ERJ 135/145, launched at the Paris Air Show 1989, was an evolution of the Brasilia, again with 2+1 seating, but a pure jet with engines at the rear. It was to be the first Embraer to operate scheduled services into London City Airport. Including Chinese assembled aircraft and the Legacy corporate version 1,225 have been completed.

Embraer into the 21st century

In 2000, Embraer was listed on the New York Stock Exchange with the Government shareholding minimal.

On 29 October 2001 the prototype Embraer E-Jet was rolled out at São José dos Campos amongst much pomp and ceremony. On hand to share the limelight with the charismatic Embraer Chairman Maurício Botelho was Moritz Suter, then Chief Executive of London City Airport operator Crossair.

Embraer had arrived with the big boys with an aircraft that had no direct rival. Little were we to know then that the E-Jet would become in a few short years numerically the largest aircraft at London City Airport, not under a Crossair (later to become part of SWISS) banner, but British Airways.

At the time of writing the combined order book for the original series and the new improved E-Jet E2 family stands at around 1,750 aircraft. It is it the world's largest selling small regional jet.

Two variants of the aircraft are approved at London City Airport, the E170 and the larger E190. Only British Airways flies the smaller plane offering 76 seats at a seat pitch of 30 inches. Alitalia and KLM also operate the E190 from the airport. All offer 98–100 seats on the E190 in a 2+2 configuration with slightly more space between the seats than on the E170. The British Airways summer service to the Greek island of Santorini is by far the longest non-stop route, 3 hours and 30 minutes and 1,600 miles.

The fly-by-wire aircraft required no physical modification to perform the approach. The cockpit has a simple switch which commands the number four and five outer wing spoilers to offset slightly while the control column is in a neutral position, creating the drag required to increase the rate of descent. Passengers hardly notice the increased descent angle, which is 5.5 degrees in order to meet noise restrictions, compared to 3 degrees normally.

With a very healthy order book for the original aircraft Embraer announced in November 2011 it would be developing revamped versions of the E-Jet family, later to be called the E2. By 2020 when both the original aircraft and its successor will be flying out of London City Airport passengers will never notice that the aircraft have different engines, the original E-Jet powered by General Electric CF34 and the new machine with a pair of Pratt & Whitney 1000G geared turbofans. Embraer says the E2 will offer 16–24% lower fuel burn and maintenance reduced by 15–25%.

The E190-E2 took its first flight on 23 May 2016 with the prototype one of the stars of Farnborough 2016. By mid-summer 2017 four pre-production aircraft (three E190-E2 and one E190) have accumulated over 700 hours of test flying.

The initial E190-E2 jet is on schedule to be delivered in the first half of 2018 and the launch operator will be Widerøe, the largest Norwegian regional airline. At present they are not a London City Airport customer but its main hub, Oslo Airport, Gardermoen, is within easy reach of London with the new aircraft. At LCY the E190-E2 is expected to offer around 100 seats, the same as the earlier model, but with the 195, not an LCY aircraft, a 144-passenger configuration will be the maximum, a 20-seat increase over the earlier aircraft.

For British Airways, the new aircraft could allow for a full complement of passengers to the Greek islands and also possibly The Canaries.

The fly-by-wire system has been revamped but a noticeable feature in the cabin are much larger overhead bins, a 40% increase. The real giveaway is the longer wingspan for the E190-E2 (33.7m versus 28.72m). At London City Airport and its rather tight apron space, only the new easterly extension will accommodate the aircraft. It is nearly as wide as the Airbus A318 (34.1m), only the Bombardier CS100 is broader (35.1m).

One very interesting feature of the new E2 is the Panasonic inflight entertainment and connectivity (IFEC) system offering streaming entertainment and wi-fi connectivity services. Passengers can enjoy on-board movies, music, news, and in-cabin services through seat back screens or their own personal devices. The system supports Windows, Mac OS, and iOS devices, as well as browsers including Internet Explorer, Safari, Chrome and Firefox.

The E2 has accrued 275 firm orders, in addition to 415 options, purchase rights, and letters-of-intent, totalling 690 commitments from airline customers and leasing companies. Currently, July 2017, the E-Jets are operating with about 70 customers in 50 countries, being the global leader in the segment of aircraft with up to 130 seats, with over 50% market share.

This is the brand-new Embraer 190 E2 on a test flight in Brazil. It will offer greater range and more destinations for the future.

Canada – de Havilland and Bombardier

The Dash 7 was developed by the Canadian aerospace company de Havilland Canada (DHC) during the 1970s when it was perceived (wrongly as it turned out) that with the success of the Dash 6 (Twin Otter) there was a market for a 50-seat aircraft with STOL (short take-off and landing) capabilities. De Havilland Canada was an offshoot (1928) of the British aircraft manufacturer and was later to go on to produce the indigenous, and very successful Chipmunk (DHC1), plus assembling many designs by others typified by the de Havilland Mosquito. Of the 4,005 produced 1,747 were built in Canada.

In 1974 de Havilland Canada was nationalised and later sold to Boeing, who themselves disposed of what was an ailing company to its current Canadian owners, Bombardier.

The 19-seat utility Twin Otter was produced from 1966 until 1988, with Brymon Airways the first UK operator. At one time it operated ten of them. In 2006 Viking Air of Victoria, British Columbia, purchased the type certificates from Bombardier Aerospace for all the out-of-production de Havilland Canada aircraft (DHC1 through DHC7) and resurrected the 'Twotter'. As the very much updated Viking Twin Otter 400 it is still produced in limited numbers, serial number 1,000 now not that far off. Loganair in Scotland took delivery of a pair of brand new Viking Twin Otters in 2015, over 40 years since the arrival of the first de Havilland Canada machine in the UK.

From the Twin Otter (DHC6) it was on to the Dash 7 (DHC7). This was to sell only 113 units with the final aircraft off the production line bound for Eurocity Express and London City Airport. There are thought to be around 40 still in service.

But for the Dash 7 there probably would not be a London City Airport.

The four-engined aircraft was designed as a regional airliner capable of operating from strips as short as 640m at Unst in the Outer Hebrides, Brymon and Britain's most northerly destination. It was meant to serve small city centre airports which London City came to typify, where noise requirements were particularly strict, and featured four slow-turning props to cut noise. The problem for de Havilland Canada was that London City Airport is a rarity. City centre airports have never caught on, Sheffield City in the UK lasting some five years as a scheduled operation from 1998 to 2002, and Berlin's historic Tempelhof forced to close.

The Dash 7 made its maiden flight in March 1975 with Rocky Mountain Airlines taking the first aircraft in February 1978. In early September of that year it made its true international debut at the Farnborough Air Show and potential buyers were invited to fly in it, including the author with his Brymon Airways hat on.

The first UK Twin Otter over Toronto, with Tom Appleton in charge.

We were all impressed, no more so than Bill Bryce, owner of the airline. Bryce was building up a fleet of Twin Otters operating out of what was not much more than a field called Roborough Airport, Plymouth. The grass main runway was asphalted and lengthened to almost 1200m allowing the Dash 7 enough range to fly to Aberdeen when fully loaded.

In order to allow the Dash 7 to achieve its excellent STOL characteristics the aircraft employs many aerodynamic devices. The wing flaps are double slotted and span approximately 75% of the trailing edge of the wing. In a typical approach the flaps will be set to 45 degrees before landing which allows for a slower approach speed (typically 70–85 knots) and steeper descent. Upon touchdown the flaps immediately return to the 25 degrees position which decreases the lift created by the wing thereby increasing braking effectiveness. The aircraft also employs two ground spoilers per wing, and two roll spoilers per wing. The roll spoilers' primary job is to augment the ailerons, however upon touchdown all four roll spoilers activate along with all four ground spoilers to spoil much of the lift generated by the wing.

While the Dash 7 proved to be a commercial failure its successor, the Dash 8, now in Bombardier Q400 form, is one of the most successful small regional airliners of all time, with over 1,200 built by the summer of 2017.

De Havilland Canada began development of the Dash 8 in the late 1970s in response to what it saw as a considerable market demand for a new generation 30- to 40-seat commuter airliners. With two engines, good but not astonishing runway performance and a 2+2 cabin width much the same as the Dash 7, it proved to be just what the small regional airlines required. Unlike the earlier aircraft's single back door, it was provided with access from both the front and rear making for quicker turnarounds.

Thirty-seat, 50-seat and later a 78-seat passenger version were produced. This largest aircraft, enhanced as the Q400, is still in production.

Like the Dash 7, the Dash 8 features a high mounted wing and T-tail, an advanced flight control system and large full length trailing edge flaps. Power is supplied by two Pratt & Whitney Canada turboprops. The first flight of the first of two pre-production aircraft was on 20 June 1983, with Canadian certification awarded on 28 September 1984. The first customer delivery was to NorOntair of Canada on 23 October 1984.

Bombardier is a long-established Canadian engineering company founded by Joseph-Armand Bombardier in 1942 and perhaps best known around the world for its rail industry skills, with a major production unit in Derby (UK). It ventured into aerospace acquiring business jet manufacturer Canadair in 1986, Northern Ireland's Short Brothers in 1989, Learjet a year later and finally de Havilland Aircraft of Canada in 1992.

In 1992, Bombardier put into production its CRJ series of regional jets, the aircraft a development of the Canadair Challenger executive jet. Both, in much developed form, continue in production.

By 1996 the Dutch Fokker company was in financial trouble. The Fokker 50 turboprops were the second most popular aircraft at London City Airport behind the BAe 146/Avro jet. Fokker went into bankruptcy and its series of small rear-engined jets (100 seats and less) died with it. It did not have the financial muscle to develop them further. What was required was a 21st century medium range maximum 130-seat aircraft that could sell all around the world. Operating into the highly prestigious London City Airport would be a bonus. Embraer and Bombardier took up the cudgels with the Brazilian company introducing the EMB 170 in 2007 to the airport.

Bombardier were slow off the mark, first of all looking at Fokker and later at Dornier, whose twin-engined Avro look-alike rolled out but was never to fly. Airbus tried to compete with the A318 offering 130 seats (and 32 seats in a special business-class only aircraft at London City) but with only 69 in current service it never sold in the volume the European consortium needed. Boeing produced a variant on the 737 called the 600, but it fared no better with around the same number of sales.

Finally Bombardier announced a five-seat abreast C Series at the Farnborough Airshow in July 2004 to replace ageing DC9/MD-80, Fokker 100, Boeing 737 Classic and BAe/Avro 146, with 20% lower operating costs.

The smaller version would carry 110–115 passengers and the larger one 130–135 passengers over 3,200 nautical miles. It was just that little bit larger than the Embraers in terms of passenger numbers and could fly slightly further. Options of 2+2 and 3+2 could be offered versus 2+2 only from the South American aircraft.

The company talked about entry into service by 2010. Economic conditions around the world were declining, but a small design team continued to develop the project in the mid-2000s. Bombardier kept their thoughts to themselves and with private discussions continuing at some airlines the marketing efforts more or less dried up.

On 13 July 2008, in a press conference on the eve of the opening of that year's Farnborough Air Show, Bombardier Aerospace formally launched the C Series, with a letter of interest from Lufthansa for 60 aircraft, including 30 options. The final assembly of the aircraft would be at Mirabel, Montreal, with the project truly international and major component suppliers from around the world including Northern Ireland (Belfast), France and Italy. China was the home for much of the fuselage with Pratt & Whitney the engine supplier. There would be two variants, the CS100 with a maximum of 135 seats and the CS300 with 148 comfortable seats or 160 at a push.

The vast majority of current Airbus Neo and Boeing 737 MAX start with 180 seats.

The Bombardier C Series aircraft contains a high usage of composite material and bigger windows than usual. It features large, rotating overhead storage bins, allowing each passenger to stow a sizeable carry-on bag overhead.

The first C Series, a CS100, was delivered to Swiss International Air Lines (commonly called SWISS) on 29 June 2016 at Montreal-Mirabel International Airport and began revenue flights on 15 July 2016 with a service between Zurich and Paris. In August 2016, SWISS reported 'much higher' reliability than other new aircraft, citing the Airbus A380, A320neo and Boeing 787, with an airline spokesperson stating: 'The customer feedback is very positive with the expected remarks concerning the bright cabin, reduced noise, enough leg room and space for hand luggage as well as the comfortable seats. Also the feedback from our pilots is gratifying. They especially like the intuitive flying experience.'

The first operator of the CS300 was Latvian carrier airBaltic in December 2016.

Flybe is the largest operator of the Bombardier Q400 at LCY.

In March 2017, Bombardier conducted steep approach landings at London City Airport with the second prototype CS100, receiving Transport Canada and European Aviation Safety Agency (EASA) steep approach certification in April 2017. It is the largest aircraft ever to operate into the airport.

On 26 March 2017 London City Airport reached another landmark with the successful flight of a CS100 to New York John F. Kennedy Airport (JFK) carrying a representative payload. Bombardier says a transatlantic CS100 would be configured with about 40 modular flat-bed seats.

The flight to JFK took just over seven hours with something less than two hours of fuel remaining. British Airways' current service via Shannon has a 9hr 25min scheduled time and 7hr 25min for the return non-stop. At Heathrow, carriers advertise around 7hr 40min going west and 6hr 50min in the other direction. British Airways' London City fares are common-rated with Heathrow. The airport noted, once again, that the taxiing time at London City Airport is significantly shorter than other major airports and planes tend to get a 'straight in approach' and no holding. Even from New York, passengers can be on the DLR easily within 15 minutes of actually landing. London City to New York is 3,466 miles.

The inaugural SWISS CS100 flight between Zurich and Manchester took place on 16 July 2016. Here follows part of the *Business Travel News (BTN)* report.

'Regular SWISS travellers will be delighted to see the same layout, 2+3, similar 30/32 inch pitch, plus wider (18.5 and 19 inch) and much more comfortable seats, which also slightly recline. Innovations include a huge overhead storage bin, ideal for operations where the majority of customers will have carry-on luggage, and extra-large windows measuring 11 x 16 inch, positioned high on the sidewall to provide an optimal viewing angle and natural light. They are nearly as big as those on the Boeing 787, although offering sliding blinds rather than the sophisticated dimmers on the Dreamliner. A one-piece folding table comes out of the seatback, which also has a pair of holdalls for water or beer, or both! Novel is a small individual screen showing the usual flight information and maps, plus a safety note which lights when a seatbelt is advised.

'From a passenger point of view, the new aircraft is a delight, giving a much better ambience than the competing, and smaller, Embraer E series (2+2) and offering a cabin height of 83 inches against 79 inches.'

Bombardier may have found a niche in the marketplace for an aircraft that does not really have a competitor, with a maximum 135 seats (CS100) or up to 160 seats with the CS300. The new Embraer E2 will appeal to established E series operators but is essentially a size smaller.

A recent order by Delta Air Lines for 75 CS100 would indicate that the Montreal-based company is not competing with Airbus/Boeing, whose A320neo and 737 MAX are another size up, starting from 150 seats. The smallest Airbus, the 132-seat A318, is now well out of production, with the 69 noted in airline service, including the British Airways Club World business class operation from London City via Shannon to New York JFK. Depending on seat layout the CS100 has both Moscow and the Gulf states well within range.

Markus Binkert, Chief Commercial Officer of SWISS, spoke at Zurich Airport before departure: 'I am extremely proud that we are the first airline in the world to put this totally newly-developed aircraft into service,' he said. 'The Bombardier CS100 is a class act in every respect: comfort, economics and environmental credentials. And its service entry today ushers in a new era in short- and medium-haul air travel.'

BTN agreed. 'Passengers will like the new aircraft. However, it is up to the airline bean counters to make sure it works economically. We all adored Concorde.'

To date Bombardier has racked up 360 firm orders including the 75 for Air Canada (CS100). These include 20 for airBaltic (CS300), 10 CS100 plus 20 CS300 for the Lufthansa Group (all for SWISS), 10 for Korean Air (CS300). Porter Airlines of Toronto, a successful Q400 customer, would also like to operate the aircraft from Billy Bishop Toronto City Airport, in many ways a copy of London City Airport. The airport is a political 'hot potato', perhaps motivated by Toronto Pearson International Airport who see it as a competitor. A plus point is that the local Bombardier plant assembles the Q400 and manufactures parts for the C Series.

First landing. In August 2017 SWISS inaugurated Bombardier CS100 flights between LCY and Zurich.

The Also Rans
by Ian Harbison

Ian Harbison is one of the UK's most experienced aviation journalists. Now specialising in aircraft maintenance with MRO Management, and interiors with Aircraft Cabin Management, he was Editor of Regional Airline World magazine from 1990 to 2000. Here, he looks at some of the other aircraft types that have appeared at the airport over the years.

There are the regional aircraft that gained approval to operate into London City Airport (LCY) and the ones that ended up in regular service. Part of the reason for the discrepancy is that, during the 1990s, when a number of new projects were launched, the airport was seen as something of a 'Holy Grail' that would help sales, so clearance became part of the flight test development programme. This was particularly so after the runway extension opened in March 1992.

Just a month later, the airport held an Open Day, where manufacturers were able to display their newly approved aircraft to potential customers. These included the ATR 42, BAe ATP and 146, de Havilland Canada Dash 8 Series 100 and the Saab 340. In the end, the ATP and Saab 340 were never used at the airport.

Fokker 50

The Fokker 50 was designed by the Dutch manufacturer in the 1980s as a replacement for its venerable F-27 Friendship that started production in 1958. The earlier aircraft had excellent short field performance and the wide and sturdy undercarriage allowed operations from unprepared strips, with the result that it found favour with airlines in many underdeveloped countries. That level of field performance was retained by the Fokker 50, making London City clearance an easy option.

However, the new aircraft could take advantage of subsequent developments in technology. This included extensive use of composite materials, large-scale use of hot-bonded structures and comprehensive anti-corrosion treatment, giving it an economic repair life of 90,000 landings.

The Pratt & Whitney Canada PW127 turboprop engines offered significantly lower fuel consumption than the Rolls-Royce Darts of the F-27 and, in combination with slow-turning, six-bladed propellers, achieved external noise levels up to 18 EPNdB below Chapter 3 requirements. This was augmented internally by vibration dampers in the structure to give extremely low noise levels in the cabin, typically below 77 dB(A) through large parts of the cabin (depending on flight stage). The cabin cross section is also comparable to the Dash 7 and Dash 8, with a 2+2 seating configuration.

Another technological advance was a full glass cockpit from Honeywell.

The aircraft flew for the first time on 28 December 1985 and the initial delivery just over a year later. Production ceased in 1997 after a total of 208 Fokker 50s had been built. Unfortunately, the last few were completed after the company's bankruptcy in 1996. During that time, the aircraft was selected by the regional associates of many major European airlines, such as KLM, Lufthansa and SAS, as the aircraft's capacity, between 50 and 56 seats, was ideal for these operations. However, it was not until 1993 that the first of the type began to operate at London City.

This was the launch of services by VLM, a new Belgian carrier based in Antwerp. Typical of the niche markets generated by airports like London City, the international diamond trade was one source of regular passengers. The airline did well, adding destinations and aircraft while offering a high degree of service. The airline was taken over in 2007 by Air France KLM and two years later, it was merged with CityJet, also an Air France KLM subsidiary. In 2010, the VLM name disappeared and the Fokker 50s continued to fly in CityJet colours until they were retired.

Other airlines to operate the Fokker 50 at London City were KLM Cityhopper and Luxair.

The company also gained approval for its Fokker 100 twinjet and, by extension, the smaller Fokker variant but these never saw commercial service at London City.

Crossair Saab 2000 and getting airborne a VLM Fokker 50.

Dornier

Initially, the Dornier 228 was the only other aircraft apart from the Dash 7 to be approved. This followed a successful demonstration in 1987 by small Dutch operator Flexair. CEO Carlo Englebert had links through his other business ventures with the airport's then owners, Mowlem, and the first flights were charters ferrying specialist workers in support of construction projects in London. Outside demand grew to the point where scheduled services could begin in 1989. Performance limitations meant that the toilet had to be removed, but it was not important on short routes to Rotterdam and Amsterdam where Englebert persuaded the Schiphol authorities to allow him to use the executive terminal, in many ways replicating the LCY experience. Services continued until 1994 when the airline went out of business.

Following the 228 came the 328, a 30-seat aircraft that was available as a turboprop or as a jet. This was used by Suckling Airways, which evolved into Scot Airways. Today, the 328 Jet is still in use, with SUN-AIR of Denmark (operating as a BA franchise).

Saab 2000

This 50-seater, powered by two powerful Rolls-Royce (originally Allison) AE 2100 turboprops for high speed, was pretty much designed around the needs of Crossair, which later became SWISS in an unusual takeover by a regional airline of a national flag carrier. Crossair was led by the charismatic Moritz Suter, who demanded that the Saab 2000 be capable of operating into restricted airports, although he also had in mind Lugano in southern Switzerland as another key destination, the airport having a steep approach requirement and lying in a valley between mountains.

He also commanded that the aircraft had a window in the forward toilet, which required some late redesign by the Swedish manufacturer. Major modifications to the elevator control system and horizontal tailplane to solve handling problems were the main reasons for a delay of almost a year before Crossair received its first aircraft in 1994. In addition, a noise 'hot spot' in the cabin meant that an active noise control system had to be fitted.

Today it appears at LCY in the colours of Skywork, a Swiss airline, and Eastern Airways, another BA franchise.

Above: *Eastern Airways from Newcastle was an operator of the Jetstream 41 for a short while.*

Right: *Not as popular as the competing Bombardier Q400 at London City, but a bigger overall seller, Aurigny flew the ATR 72 to Guernsey.*

Jetstream 41

Another aircraft that made a brief appearance was the British Aerospace Jetstream 41. This 29-seat stretch of the 19-seat Jetstream 31, powered by two Honeywell TPE-331 turboprops, was operated by British Regional Airlines (BRAL) as a British Airways franchise from London City to Sheffield City. Unfortunately, this small airport was never really successful and was closed down in 2002 after four years of operation.

ATR 42/72

The ATR 42 appeared at the 1992 London City Airport Open Day but did not return for some time on scheduled airline services. That is slightly surprising, as a glance at the customer list shows that the aircraft is ideally suited for smaller airports, especially those on islands. It was flown by Air France (Brit Air), Air Wales and Eurowings in the early 2000s but nowonly Flybe continues to operate the aircraft. There is a trend towards bigger planes if a service is a success. The ATR bucks the trend. The larger ATR 72 made brief appearances with Aurigny and Aer Arann. The ATR 42 is currently flown by Blue Islands, the Jersey-based carrier, under a Flybe franchise.

And into the next decade

For the future the Embraer E-Jet-E2 and Bombardier C Series will clearly be the mainstay into the next decade but also possible are the Sukhoi Superjet SS100 (Russia), which has recently been upgraded with more powerful engines, Antonov 148 (Ukraine), Comac ARJ21 (China) and Mitsubishi Regional Jet (Japan).

Inevitably, over such a long period of time, aircraft types come and go. If there is one distinct trend, it is that capacity increases to match market demand for airline services direct to the heart of London. While there is a natural cap on the size of aircraft, dictated by runway length, it has become clear that manufacturers still continue to see London City Airport as a challenge to be met and a useful commercial opportunity.

Chapter Eleven
A Heavy SWISS Landing

Sinking, Floating, Flying

A hard landing at London City Airport resulted in an imaginative response to getting the aircraft back into service. Ian Harbison reported thus in MRO Management in 2008.

As is well known, London City is an extremely restricted airport. Built in the middle of the old commercial docks on the River Thames, it has a single runway just 1199m in length and requires a steeper 5.5-degree approach, limiting it to specially approved aircraft flown by specially certified pilots. However, the most difficult part of any landing is the transition from the approach angle to the flare just before landing, as the aircraft rotates to a nose-up angle.

On 18 August 2007, an Avro RJ100 of SWISS was just at this point, about 50 feet above the ground, when the wind changed from a slight headwind to a slight tailwind. The loss of lift caused the aircraft to suddenly sink. The crew's instinctive reaction was to pull back on the controls, but this resulted in a nose-high attitude of 9.5 degrees that caused the aircraft's rear fuselage to briefly strike the runway.

Although the aircraft was taxied to the stand and the 88 passengers and five crew disembarked safely, an inspection revealed that significant structural damage had occurred to the lower fuselage in the area of the aft cargo hold. The damage was repairable and, as the aircraft was only seven years old, the repairs would be economically viable. It could not be safely flown back to base in Switzerland or even to the nearest maintenance facility. With limited parking available on the ramp, the space taken up by the aircraft was causing concern to the airport's management.

SWISS decided to contact BAE Systems Regional Aircraft's Field Support Organisation, which dispatched a team from its repair design office to assess the damage. This turned out to include scrape marks along the lower fuselage for almost 12 feet with varying degrees of cracking on nine fuselage frames. Most of those

Above: *Nine of the fuselage frames had to be replaced.*

Opposite, Top to Bottom:
A temporary hangar was erected on the north side of the Royal Albert Dock.

The first, and hopefully last, floating Avro RJ100.

Home from home for the engineers. Any bad weather problems were forgotten.

had suffered some buckling or distortion, while all the horizontal stringers in the damaged area also showed distortion.

The answer was the construction of a temporary hangar which in fact came from Support Air (UK) on the Albert Dock quayside.

On 10 September, SWISS said that it had taken the innovative decision to contract Carillion Marine to provide a 400-tonne flattop pontoon to float the aircraft from the airport across the water to a neighbouring dock – where a temporary hangar facility would be erected – and asked Regional Aircraft to propose a permanent repair. These pontoons are generally used as marine working platforms for piling operations (Carillion had earlier been involved in piling for a runway extension at London City). The selected pontoon was chosen for its deck area and stability and, as it could carry a 170-tonne crane, the weight of the aircraft was not a major concern. In fact, as the aircraft was towed onboard and rolled into position, the pontoon hardly moved in the water.

In parallel, the airline also contracted with Support Air (UK) to provide a temporary hangar to house the aircraft and the repair working party, complete with lighting, ventilation, stores and other accessories as required by the client. The hangar was erected on waste ground on an old dock to the north of the airport which had recently been used as a temporary runway for the London leg of the Red Bull Air Race World Series.

The scope of the permanent EASA certified repair entailed the manufacture or procurement of structure and consumable items, the rework of the existing aircraft structure to allow the fitment of the repair, the installation process, reprotection of the new internal structure, full EASA-compliant documentation for the repair and full BAE Systems paperwork to support a SWISS application for a permit to fly, if required. This was accepted by the airline, which also stipulated that the company should act as full integrator for the repair to include all logistical aspects. This allowed the customer to focus on the daily operations of running the airline and not to be distracted with the repair of one of its aircraft.

Regional Aircraft created a fully integrated team to manage the programme. Project management was run from the company's Prestwick facility in Scotland while an on-site field service support team managed a team from Chevron Technical Services, a specialist in BAe 146/RJ maintenance based at Kemble in the UK, which provided skilled labour as part of its EASA Part 145 approved subcontractor status.

Spares and procurement support was provided by Prestwick and also the Weybridge

The return barge trip proved to be much easier than the outbound.

Spares Logistics Centre. Some 325 line items had to be sourced for the repair and of this some 75% were available from the outset. Fifty line items had to be manufactured and, in total, more than 600 individual components had to be found, a major logistical exercise.

Start date for the repair was 1 October and it was estimated, based on previous experience, that it would take 10 weeks to complete the job, using a double shift pattern of approximately 10 to 12 people. The first task was to ensure that the aircraft was completely level at all times to maintain perfect alignment of the structure as it was reassembled. As the hangar had been constructed on a piece of rough ground, steel beams were placed through windows on either side of the aircraft to support it.

By the end of October, replacement of all the major frame sections had been completed and, during November, the new keel skin had been positioned and secured. By 21 November, the repair had been completed and the aircraft was powered up. Handover back to SWISS took place two days later. The airline then carried out the reverse barging operation back to London City Airport, which was carried out during the quiet weekend period.

The full repair had been achieved, negating the need for a permit to fly. After some minor maintenance on the ramp, the aircraft was flown back to Switzerland on 4 December. In total, the repair had taken nine weeks and had been completed within timescales and within budget.

Chapter Twelve

New York to London City Airport

New York to London City Airport with a stop

Back in late 2005 British Airways came up with the idea of instigating flights from London City Airport to New York John F. Kennedy (JFK). A refuelling stop would be required east to west due to headwinds but all the possible aircraft could make it non-stop in the other direction.The thinking behind the project was perhaps two-fold. Air France was rumoured to be considering such an operation with the new US – Europe bilateral approved and the EU Freedom of the Skies gave no licensing problems. It would be a fine way of promoting British Airways whole London City Airport operation flown by CityFlyer.

British Airways quickly moved ahead.

As far as the general public was concerned BA would offer a high visibility route to New York. This would add to the dozen or so CityFlyer (BA branded) flights to the United Kingdom and mainland European destinations that were flown at the time.The publicity department came up with the flight numbers BA001 outbound and BA002 return, the same as the much-loved Concorde.

Shannon was chosen as the stopover with passengers deplaning and passing through the US pre-clearance, allowing for a domestic arrival at New York and a quick departure, luggage permitting, at New York JFK Terminal 7. It was clear that most passengers would be business people who travel light and want to be away at speed on arrival.

Airbus was the obvious aircraft supplier with the A320 series the mainstay of the BA fleet. Crewing could be out of Heathrow for the flight deck, a small band of pilots checked out for the London City Airport steep approach but also available for normal duties. Gatwick would be the base for the cabin staff.

In March 2006, the European Aviation Safety Agency (EASA) certified a modified control software enhancement to the Airbus A318 designed to allow the aircraft to perform steep approaches. The software adapts the control systems of the aircraft when the steep approach function is selected by the crew, by automatically deploying some of the spoiler panels to provide additional drag when the aircraft is in the landing configuration. It also provides alternative aural alerts to the crew and modifies spoiler deployment automatically below 120 feet on landing. The A318 steep approach procedure allows the aircraft to perform approaches at descent angles of up to 5.5 degrees, as opposed to the standard 3 degrees for a normal landing. The steep, quieter approach was part of the airport's planning approval.

British Airways Airbus A318 interior – British Airways operates with three cabin staff to look after 34 passengers.

The only private lounge within the terminal at LCY – For the daily New York service.

A test flight was conducted in May 2006 to prove the aircraft's capability at London City Airport.The test flight also confirmed the aircraft's compatibility with the limited manoeuvring and parking space at LCY. Subsequently, in August 2009 Airbus delivered the first of two LCY adapted A318s to British Airways, which began operating the route the following month.

Originally BA offered two services Monday to Friday and a Saturday outbound and an overnight Sunday from New York. With the US authorities reducing the opening hours of the Shannon facility in early 2016, for the second flight passengers had to try their luck at New York Border Control with their long queues. One of the benefits of the service was gone and the second outbound was cancelled.

British Airways has been clever with the revised timetable and now operates Monday to Thursday outbound at 09:40 with arrival, on a Friday at 12:40 local, and on Sunday just as the airport opens at 12:35 getting in at 17:00. Travellers on the Friday and Sunday flights need to go through the full formalities at JFK. Flight time is scheduled at 9 hours and 15 minutes, two hours longer than Heathrow.

In the other direction, it is non-stop 7 hours 25 minutes, 15 minutes more than Heathrow but no aircraft taxiing and a very quick access to transport. From Kennedy, the full BA lounge facilities are available with departure 18:30 every day and an early morning arrival into London scheduled just before 07:00. You can easily be in the City by 08:00 and there is also a courtesy chauffeur service to the nearby Radisson Blu (Edwardian) where a complimentary breakfast and spa facilities are offered.

Here I paraphrase a journey made several years ago to New York when the service was twice daily and brought up to date in terms of the current schedule.

'British Airways prestige London City (LCY) – Kennedy New York (JFK) service has been operating now for nearly a decade. Inaugurated in August 2009 the six times per week flight uses a pair of specially adopted Airbus A318 offering 32 lie-flat seats in a 2+2 configuration. It is a great way to fly to New York in spite of the Shannon stopover.

I flew the service last week, outward bound over the former Olympic Park, now named after Queen Elizabeth II. Fabulous views.

The passengers seemed a very mixed bag. Business travellers appropriately dressed and others with more relaxed attire. One couple I spoke to were retired and off to New York for a holiday. They were trying the service 'for fun'. It was 'thumbs up' as we got off. Another gentleman was based in Canary Wharf and Essex and said it was, for him, the only way to Kennedy. An American was trying it for the first time.

The London City fare structure is the same as Heathrow and if it is the Avios scheme you use do get in as soon as the bookings open as the number of seats available is very limited. You can also go one way Heathrow and the other London City. The BA ticketing is fully flexible. It all rather depends on your travel requirements, origination and final destination. The route is also an alternative to and from New York for many of the lesser mainland Europe airports that do not service JFK direct but offer LCY services. It is far quicker to change at City than alternative airports.

The service is a success, but for unusual reasons. Clearly it does not make any money but that is tiny in the scheme of things. It is a prestige operation that 'flies the flag'. CAA statistics show a maximum of 24,000 passengers in 2014 which would indicate a two-way load factor in the mid-sixties. There were only 20 of us on this flight. In total five crew and a purpose-built aircraft, managing a very healthy 4,500 flying hours per year with just three landings per day.

The stopover in Shannon takes about 30 minutes on the ground with a requirement to go through US Border Control within the terminal building. If you have hold luggage that must be claimed and nominally inspected. Once through the US Border Control at Shannon passengers are technically in America.

London City–New York is a very prestigious route, has excellent publicity value, and serves the Canary Wharf and East London market. From, say, The Bank the airport journey time is 22 minutes with a service every ten minutes. If you have strong nerves you can catch the DLR at just after 08:30 and be ready to get airborne at 09:30. Officially it is a 15-minute check-in. From the same starting point allow up to two hours to Heathrow by car, or say a 30-minute taxi ride to Paddington and the Heathrow Express, or change at Holborn and take the Piccadilly Line. And allow plenty of time for getting to the gate. Add at least another 30 minutes if you want to use the lounge.

At London City Airport there is a dedicated New York check-in, one of the best organised mechanised security operations around and the boarding gate is the lounge. There was a selection of cold meat and smoked fish, fruit, yoghurt and pastries. Hard and soft drinks. No matter how late you are something quick can be grabbed. It is all reminiscent of the old Concorde lounge ambience.

The main airside waiting area at London City Airport has been continuously updated, has all the Duty Free and ancillary sales outlets needed, and also various eating places if you arrive early.

No air bridges at London City and it is a short walk to the aircraft steps. One assumes if it is

Copying the original Heathrow Terminal 4 Concorde concept a gate lounge at LCY offers canapes and drinks.

raining an umbrella, with perhaps an escort, is provided.

Drinks are not served on boarding but your jacket is taken and stored away as per normal Club World.

Once on board the lounge atmosphere is retained, a sort of private members' club. Three cabin staff but it is pre-packaged meals on BA 001 (Concorde only offered high class canapes), the first course served on the London – Shannon leg. There is a choice but it is limited although you can pre-order the whole range of BA special meals. It is nothing fancy, a rather uprated Club Europe experience, albeit in a much nicer setting.

The 2+2 fully lie-flat seat has a reset button. It will adjust for the ideal dining position, the button marked with knives and forks. But you have to climb across your seat partner if that person is in the lie flat mode.

Another unique oddity is a sign in the overhead panel which tells you when the mobile connection system is functioning. The seat had two personal power points that can accept UK, EU and US plugs without the need for an adaptor.

OnAir have provided an SMS (text) and MMS (multi-media) system that links seamlessly with both Blackberry and iPhone hand-helds. You can link these into a laptop too, or use a dongle. Email could not be easier and is inexpensive. Text costs 50p per message and is free incoming. Surfing the web can be very expensive. BA, as a matter of policy, does not allow phone calls. For entertainment and information purposes iPads are supplied, very easy to use, sitting comfortably on the cocktail table provided.

There are not many places to put things but a newspaper storage bin is provided. There is a lavatory at either end and a cleverly integrated crew rest area.

On the leg out of Shannon the second and third courses are served. Then there is time to stretch out and use the full six feet lie-flat bed. It is as good as any on a narrow-bodied aircraft but not the same as per long-haul services. No real privacy and a small divider at head level. Standard blankets and pillows. I grabbed some sleep and woke to spectacular views as we flew over Greenland.

About 90 minutes before landing, afternoon tea was offered. Not very attractive sandwiches and the normal, very pleasant BA scones. But feeling full from the excellent luncheon steak I had to pass on the selection of cakes.

How to summarize the London City – New York service?

I for one thoroughly enjoyed it and would use again.

The big problem is that the flight is now only daily and had I gone by taxi and got stuck in traffic I would have had a serious problem, the only alternative back to Heathrow, or in desperation via Amsterdam or Frankfurt. From New York it is far easier with plenty of both British Airways and partner American Airlines services available if the flight is missed.

Although the service is not as good as long-haul Club World, I really enjoyed my BA001 flight. It certainly felt very exclusive and as close to a private jet as you can get. The extra time taken to get to New York was worth it to have such a hassle-free immigration process and quick exit from JFK. I would certainly consider this service again when going to JFK. For the return the early landing was perfect and well rested I was able to make a City appointment near the Bank of England via DLR well in advance of my host who had struggled in for over an hour! He was also impressed! Roll on non-stop flights both ways'.

Flat bed BA A318.

It's All About Retail!

When the London City Airport first opened 30 years ago the retail outlets were very limited, both landside and airside. You could change money, have a cup of coffee, and buy a newspaper. And that was it.

Today as you enter the airport from the DLR on the left hand side there is Costa, a good place for either a quiet rendezvous, or just for meeting up before the hassle and bustle of the airport.

In the terminal proper there are a further, more or less essential, outlets with on your immediate left an information desk.

Once through security if your wait is of any time there is a choice of eateries and a good selection for those who either need essentials or are in for a retail therapy burst.

Before Security:
Panopolis
Pret A Manger
Travelex
W H Smith
The pop-up space on the left as you enter the terminal hosts temporary retailers.

After Security:
Aelia Duty Free
AeroSpa (West Pier)
Boots
Brick Lane Brews Café-bar (West Pier)
Café Nero
City Bar and Restaurant
Dixons Travel
Expressamente Illy
Jo Malone
Ladurée
Panopolis
Pilots Bar & Kitchen
Pret A Manger (West Pier)
Travelex
Tumi
WH Smith

July 2017

***Above Left:** Panopolis landside at the airport.*

***Centre Left:** Alia Duty Free in the departures lounge.*

***Left:** WH Smith is both landside and airside.*

Chapter Thirteen
London City Airport Private Jet Centre

Away from the hassle and bustle of the main terminal building on the approach road from the Connaught Bridge is the London City Airport Private Jet Centre. It could be renamed the LCY Executive Enclave as it fulfils a multi-task engagement as the only gateway for private aircraft travellers actually in London, plus a true first class service for airline customers, and a business class lounge facility for normal travellers with a little time on their hands. There is also available, upstairs, a private room, 24 square feet, capable of holding up to around a dozen people, and with all the facilities required for a small conference or meeting.

In the future, when inside the building it might be possible to hear trains rumble by sitting directly over the Elizabeth Line (Crossrail) which comes to the surface just across the road.

From the very first day it opened London City Airport offered a facility for private aircraft, but they always took second place to the scheduled traffic.

All this changed in 2002 when the then owner, Dermot Desmond, an executive jet owner himself, invested in a proper business aviation centre at the west end of the airport with its own apron area and handling service. The facility can deal with aircraft up to the size of a BAe 146/Avro (as used by Queen Elizabeth), and the large Bombardier and Gulfstream corporate jets. It has also from time to time provided a London showplace for aircraft visitors from a bygone era including a DC6 and Lufthansa's historic Junkers 52.

In aviation terminology London City Airport Private Jet Centre is called a 'Fixed Base Operation' or FBO. By road it is four miles from the Canary Wharf complex (12 minutes) and seven miles from the Bank of England (20 minutes). To the start of the A406 at its junction with the A13 and onwards to the M11/M25 is about five minutes.

The Centre's greatest claim to fame is what it calls its '90 second rule'. Customers can be in their car landside within 90 seconds of their aircraft coming to a halt on the apron and within either two or five minutes of landing, depending on the wind direction. It is also possible to be on one's aircraft within 90 seconds of coming through the facility's door and then passing

through security. All this is much appreciated by the regulars. Away from the main terminal it is all very discreet.

The Centre provides a complete corporate aviation package including various lounges, a dedicated stand for aircraft as they 'turnaround', parking for up to 20 aircraft and immigration, customs and crew facilities. Dedicated staff are on hand to provide flight planning, weather briefings and landing clearances. They also organise slot requests, ground handling arrangements, flight watch, cleaning, catering, line maintenance, refuelling, baggage and aircraft handling.

Whatever service you use, arriving at the London City Airport Private Jet Centre is rather like an entry to a five-star hotel, extremely unobtrusive, exclusive and much in favour with top businessmen, politicians and celebrities. Any paperwork is quietly dealt with as with luggage, collected from one's transport, tagged and dispatched to the aircraft.

The first class lounge in particular has the 'wow' that certain airlines' facilities offer at Heathrow. Copied perhaps from the Boeing 787 it has a privacy setting for the windows which turns them opaque at the flick of a switch. A very private small side room is available. If you want a bath or shower that is there too, or just somewhere to change. There is a range of food and drink with high quality wine and Champagne but if you need something more substantial a full menu from the main terminal can be provided. All the services expected of a high quality lounge are on hand including flat screen television, charging points and free high-speed wi-fi plus a concierge service ready to help.

Then it is through the dedicated security and short drive to your scheduled aircraft to arrive just before the door closes. The present charge is £95 per person. Inbound clients can use the privacy in reverse, including customs and immigration with baggage delivered to your transport via the airport's specialist baggage handler AirPorte to a specific destinations.

It is one way of avoiding the paparazzi.

For a private jet client it is much the same except it is the operator who pays the bill and your aircraft will either be parked directly outside the building, a very short walk, or if necessary, a chauffeured drive. Normally private jets operate with just two or three passengers although the Centre can handle up to around 30 for, say, an executive Avro.

For the business class lounge it is essentially a scaled down version of the facilities offered in first class with one essential difference. Passengers need to check-in at the main terminal from where they will be driven to the London City Airport Private Jet Centre landside. Then it is time to relax and wait to be called about 30 minutes before the flight and then another chauffeured drive to the terminal and security. For this the charge is £35. If you have time and want to relax and do some work it is perfect.

Fractional ownership, where businesses buy a percentage of an aircraft, represented in flight hours, drastically reduce the cost of private air travel and now accounts for approximately 55% of the Private Jet Centre's business. Another growth has been the sale of what used to be called 'dead legging'. A charter customer buys a one-way flight into or out of London City

Airport knowing that he must also pay for the positioning operation. Specialist brokers will often sell this leg at 'give-away' prices, an active market. Some savvy people, either to impress, or as a present, have been known to buy a flight which might finish up at, typically, Oxford Airport and continue on from that point. Not many can say they have flown on a private jet out of London City Airport.

Above and Below: Dassault Falcon 8X private jet interior and the same aircraft getting airborne.

In June 2006, the London City Airport Private Jet Centre was awarded the contract to provide a Premier Passenger Service at RAF Northolt, a contract which continues to this day. The aerodrome, famous in World War II as the base for the No. 303 Polish Fighter Squadron, perfectly complements London City for West London sitting on the A40 dual carriageway with easy access to the Hyde Park area one way, and Buckinghamshire in the other direction.

Opening hours are much the same as LCY and it is multi-functional operating as a military base and also a civil airport restricted to business aircraft only.

The big news for 2017 is the announcement by GlobeAir of a partnership with the Private Jet Centre. Claimed to be Europe's leading air taxi operator with the world's largest fleet of Citation Mustang jets, it noted a boom in business aircraft movements with a 34% increase for London-based departures from 368 in 2015 to 492 in 2016.

Chapter Fourteen
City Airport Development Plan (CADP)

On Wednesday 27 July 2016 London City Airport received planning permission for a £350 million privately funded investment which includes plans for seven new aircraft stands, a parallel taxiway and the passenger terminal extension.

The approval will enable the airport to welcome 6.5 million passengers by 2025 and inject £1.5 billion each year into the economy.

The announcement came within days of Theresa May becoming Prime Minister. Philip Hammond, the Chancellor of the Exchequer, and a former Secretary of State for Transport, and Lord Ahmad of Wimbledon, at the time Aviation Minister, made a surprise visit to the airport to give the go-ahead following formal confirmation from Transport Secretary Chris Grayling and Communities Secretary Sajid Javid.

Declan Collier, CEO, London City Airport said on the occasion:

'Today, the new Government has shown it is ready to act in the best interests of the British economy. Expansion at London City Airport will create more than 2,000 new jobs in East London, add much-needed aviation capacity in the South-East, and generate an additional £750 million per year for the UK economy. As the airport serving by far the highest proportion of business travellers in the UK (52%), who do some £11 billion of trade in Europe annually, today the Government has sent a strong message that London and the UK are very much open for business. I welcome the decision and look forward to delivering new airport capacity for the South-East by 2019.'

The development will transform the airport, one of East London's largest employers, to welcome more airlines and with it more passengers. The airport has aspirations of a Silvertown for London City Airport Elizabeth Line station.

Over the last 30 years London City Airport and its 1199m runway has become the benchmark for new quieter, next generation aircraft, larger and with a greater range. The major constraint has been runway capacity but with the introduction of a parallel taxiway landings and take-offs, known as movements in airline language, can be increased by up to 45 per hour without infringing the legal capacity of the airport. When the airport first opened 15 movements an hour was thought to be good going, but when the runway eastern holding point was added in 2003 this was more than doubled to 32. Thirty-eight movements an hour have been recorded.

The latest jet transport aircraft, such as the Bombardier CS100 have a greater wingspan than their predecessors which could restrict manoeuvrability. The increased area will alleviate this problem. Typically the Canadian aircraft, partly built in Belfast, will offer airlines the opportunity to consider longer-haul destinations including The Gulf and Middle East, Turkey, Russia and the east coast of the United States. With up to 130 passengers the throughput per aircraft

This aerial view clearly shows the extended aircraft taxiway.

Still at an early stage the plans call for an extension of the existing terminal to the east and a new 'drop off' area.

can increase by one third. They are quieter too than the previous generation.

The construction phase of development is expected to create 500 jobs and a further 1,600 posts once completed. Under the plans the airport can add approximately a further 30,000 flights by 2025, movements which are already permitted, helping to unlock more air capacity within London's airport system in advance of a new runway for the South-East of England.

Essentially there are two aspects to the development, the parallel runway and increased apron space, and the far more complex rebuilding and extending the easterly end of the existing terminal building to provide a new arrivals hall; East Pier and new aircraft stands.

The parallel taxiway development is relatively simple and involves pile driving into the dock bed thus extending the existing deck in certain locations by up to 920 feet to accommodate the terminal extension and East Pier. Seven more aircraft stands will be provided, with essentially a design evolution of the successfully refashioned original gates towards the west, and approximately a further 820 feet of taxiway to join up with the existing holding area at the eastern end of the airport. There is nothing very complicated to this engineering work except that care needs to be taken to ensure that no unknown World War II bombs found are inadvertently detonated. Most of the work will be done during normal airport operational hours although some will need to be undertaken when the airport is closed for safety reasons.

Within the last 12 months the walkway to the western gates has been extensively remodelled with an open-plan layout offering more places to sit and a bright, modern environment to enjoy, with work spaces and quiet areas. A Pret A Manger has enhanced the airside food and beverage offerings, together with Brick Lane Brews, a café/bar concept, and an airport beauty lounge, AeroSpa.

In charge of the project are the award-winning, airport architects Pascall+Watson who have been involved with London City Airport since 2011, in particular the very much modernised departure lounge. Their work includes Heathrow Terminal 2, Gatwick's revised North Terminal and a number of large airport projects in China.

While the runway and taxiway will be a highly visible creation, the largest outlay in financial terms will be the construction of the extended terminal over the existing dock. Covering over 550,000 square feet in total the extended passenger facilities will include a new baggage hall, security and border control facilities, improved retail provision, and an enlarged airside lounge area. CIP and VIP facilities for scheduled flights, currently accommodated in the Private Jet Centre, are expected to be provided. The new

Not at LCY. The new digital control operation will be at NATS HQ at Swanwick in Hampshire.

east gates will be served by an innovative pier design and walkway.

A new air traffic control tower is already on its way. It will be the first in the UK to operate as a single digital source of air traffic control and will put the airport at the forefront of a global aviation trend. The scheme is part of a safer generation of technology for air traffic management, offering increased capabilities to the controllers. The 164-feet high structure will use the latest Saab data technology to feed an operations control room based at the National Air Traffic Services (NATS) headquarters in Swanwick, Hampshire.

The digital solution is a multi-million pound investment utilising state-of-the-art 360-degree HD cameras on a newly constructed tower. A live feed with a panoramic view of the airfield, along with sensory and operational data, will be sent via super-fast secure fibre connections to a control room in Swanwick where air traffic controllers will perform their operational role, using the live footage displayed on 14 HD screens that form a seamless panoramic moving image, alongside the audio feed from the airfield, and radar readings from the skies above London, to instruct aircraft and oversee movements.

The state-of-the-art technology from Saab Digital Air Traffic Solutions, which is tried and tested and already in use at Örnsköldsvik and Sundsvall airports in Sweden, offers several advantages for efficient air traffic management at London City Airport.

Controllers will be able to utilise a range of viewing tools such as high definition zoom and enhanced visuals, which provide detailed views of activity on the airfield, including close-up views of aircraft movements along the runway, with pan-tilt zoom cameras that can magnify up to 30 times for close inspection.

They will also have real-time information, including operational and sensory data, to build an augmented reality live view of the airfield. For example, the ability to overlay the images with weather information, on-screen labels, radar data, aircraft call signs, or to track moving objects.

The sophisticated tools of a digital set-up significantly improve a controller's situational awareness, enabling quick and informed decisions that thereby offer safety and operational benefits for the airport.

The new control tower is located in the airport's long-stay car park, in line with the mid-way point of the runway, adjacent to King George V Dock. It is due to be completed in 2018, followed by more than a year of rigorous testing and training, during which the existing 30-year old tower will continue to operate. The digital tower will become fully operational in 2019.

Chapter Fifteen
London City Airport Consultative Committee (LCACC)

One of the great successes of the airport over the years has been the Consultative Committee which initially met monthly in the early years but by 1994 it was down to five annually. It has now tapered off to three or four a year as the airport has matured. The original Secretary, Stuart Innes, who had been Reg Ward's assistant in the London Docklands Development Corporation (LDDC), retired in 2015.

Besides the airport and airline users, the Consultative Committee includes representatives of the local boroughs, local authorities and public bodies, local communities and other interested parties including the Royal Docks Management Authority, Greater London Council, Metropolitan Police and the Department for Transport.

London City Airport's Consultative Committee (LCACC) is as old as the airport itself. When planning permission for the airport (then known as STOLPORT) was first given in the mid-1980s the developer, John Mowlem & Co Plc, entered into an agreement with the former LDDC, the London Borough of Newham, the Port of London Authority and the then Greater London Council. Its purpose was to regulate the environmental impact of the airport including, in particular, noise and the hours during which the airport would operate.

The agreement required the setting up of a consultative committee to 'monitor all aspects of the operation of the airport and to advise on operating procedures ... with a view to minimising noise pollution or other nuisance from whatever source'. The committee was charged also with monitoring the implementation of the agreement and to 'advise from time to time on the need for any revision thereof'. It was agreed later that the committee would also 'discuss and act on complaints from the public'.

LCACC's role is to provide a positive, inclusive and interactive forum for discussion on all matters concerning the development or operation of the airport which have an impact on the users of the airport and on people living and working in the surrounding area.

In the autumn of 1986 a Steering Group was set up to establish the Committee and the first meeting was held on 30 June 1987. In July 2012 the Committee Meeting celebrated its 25th Anniversary and the long serving contribution of its members.

Duncan Alexander, Chair of London City Airport Consultative Committee.

The LCACC Chair and Secretary positions are completely independent from the airport.

Most large airports in the UK have Consultative Committees which have their roots in the Civil Aviation Act of 1982 and subsequent issuance of Guidelines by the Secretary of State in 1996. Since 1980 the Chair and Secretary of these committees have met annually to share experience and to discuss matters of common interest. Annual meetings are hosted by a different airport each year. There are now 23 ACCs that are members of UKACCs. To be a member of UKACCs the ACC's airport must either have a passenger throughput of more than 600,000 passengers per annum or be an airport of particular regional significance. From the outset London City was considered as one of those.

For many years the Chair of LCACC, John Adshead, and the Secretary, Stuart Innes, attended the UK annual meetings.

John was invited by London City Airport to help set up the LCACC in the early 1980s. Both John and Stuart were the stalwarts of the Committee. Their commitment and reliability was commendable.

John Adshead resigned in 2016 and Duncan Alexander was appointed as Chair with George Masters as the new Secretary, whose full-time position is at the House of Lords as a Committee Assistant to the European Union Select Committee, managing the relationship between the Select Committee and its six sub-committees.

Today the LCACC meets quarterly and has two Sub-Committees; Community and Environment. Through these meetings a wide range of topics is covered including community engagement, airport development, noise and air quality and other issues impacting the local community.

Recently, for example, the issue of Uber Taxis occupying streets around the airport was reported as an increasing nuisance. The matter was raised in the sub and main Committee meetings and subsequent action was taken by the local council and the planning department to provide better staging facilities for Uber and other taxi companies. This has eased the impact on the local community but still allows a choice of surface transport to be provided. This is a good recent working example of how the LCACC strives to live up to its motto 'Community, Communication, Collaboration'.

Membership of the Committee is diverse which reflects the nature of the airport's impact on the local area. It includes representatives from local councils and surrounding boroughs, The London Development Agency, the Royal Docks Management Authority, local tenants and residents associations, the airport and airlines. In addition others are invited to attend to show their support and to hear of what are the latest developments including the local police and representatives from schools and community centres. The meetings are open to the public.

One of the key participants in the meetings is the Airport Monitoring Officer (AMO).

Newham Council and London City Airport work closely together to try to ensure that the economic advantages which arise from the operation of the airport can be maximised, and any potential problems which may adversely affect the local population can be prevented or minimised.

One of the main means of dealing with potential or actual problems is through planning controls, called Planning Conditions and S106 Agreements. Currently parts of two sets of planning controls are in force: those attached to the planning permission dated 9 July 2009 and those attached to the planning permission dated 26 July 2016. The later set will eventually fully replace the earlier one.

The controls cover a wide range of issues, including in particular noise, but also air quality and biodiversity, and sets targets for the employment of local residents.

Both sets of controls specify what is required of the airport and when a smaller number of controls apply to the council.

Both permissions include a requirement for the employment of an AMO by the Council. The AMO post was created by the 2009 agreement to ensure that the airport complies with the approved Planning Conditions.

The AMO is employed directly by Newham Council and is completely independent of the airport companies. The first AMO commenced employment with the council in 2010.

The role of the AMO can be divided into, firstly, functions relating to enforcement, should targets or standards not be met in any way, and secondly, functions relating to facilitation, whereby compliance with certain obligations, for example completion of strategies and action plans by the airport, is done in a timely and effective manner.

A summary of activity related to planning controls is reported quarterly by the AMO and within the Annual Performance Report that is published both on the airport and LCACC website.

At recent meetings regular updates have been provided on the progress with the new planning permissions and on how the airport is meeting its obligations for environmental targets, in particular noise and pollution.

The LCACC provides an important proactive link between all the stakeholders of the airport and the wider community. With the continued expansion of the airport, future links with Crossrail, local economic and residential development, its role and importance will continue to grow.

London City Airport winter 2017-2018 destinations

(Summer only routes 2017 are shown in red, but are expected to be largely the same for 2018)

(50 routes as of July 2017)

Destination	Airline
Aberdeen	Flybe
Amsterdam	British Airways, KLM/CityJet
Avignon	CityJet
Basel/Mulhouse	Skywork
Belfast City	Flybe
Bergerac	British Airways
Berlin–Tegel	British Airways
Bern	Skywork
Billund	British Airways (SUN-AIR franchise)
Cardiff	Flybe
Chambéry	British Airways
Dublin	British Airways, CityJet
Düsseldorf	British Airways
Edinburgh	British Airways, Flybe
Exeter	Flybe
Faro	British Airways
Florence	British Airways
Frankfurt	British Airways, Lufthansa
Geneva	British Airways, SWISS
Glasgow	British Airways
Granada	British Airways
Ibiza	British Airways
Isle of Man	British Airways (flown by Eastern Airlines),
Jersey	Flybe (Blue Islands franchise)
Lisbon	TAP
Luxembourg	Luxair
Mahon	British Airways
Málaga	British Airways
Menorca	British Airways
Milan–Linate	Alitalia, British Airways
Mykonos	British Airways
New York–JFK	British Airways
Nice	British Airways
Palma de Mallorca	British Airways
Paris–Orly	British Airways
Powdair	Sion
Prague	British Airways
Quimper	British Airways
Reykjavík	British Airways
Rennes	CityJet
Rome–Fiumicino	Alitalia
Rotterdam	British Airways
Santorini	British Airways
Skiathos	British Airways
Toulon	CityJet
Venice	British Airways
Zürich	British Airways, SWISS

Chapter Sixteen

Corporate Social Responsibility

London City Airport and the community

From day one London City Airport has been community conscious. This is now expressed as Corporate Social Responsibly (CSR).

The test landing at Heron Quays on 30 June 1983 was as much to gain local acceptance as to demonstrate to the Inspector the safety and practicality of the proposed airport. Mowlem was quick to brief the local public of the advantages the new airport would bring. Brymon Airways played its part too flying down from Heathrow local leaders and media highlighting the efforts made at Plymouth with industry and municipality to ensure a first-rate relationship.

The fine rapport by London City Airport with its neighbours has continued to this day with LCY now one of the largest employers in the Borough of Newham with 2,100 members of staff, 65% of which come from the local area. The Take Off Into Work job scheme, run by Newham Workplace and London City Airport to help local people into employment, has in the summer of 2017 placed over 600 people into a job at the airport.

This initiative started in 2009 with the airport getting together with the East London Business Alliance. It functions by providing work experience, job trials and classroom-based training to Newham residents to help them secure employment with many contractors on the site, and the airport itself. There are 54 concessions, airlines and other business partners.

Declan Collier, CEO of London City Airport, said: 'With the airport's focus on job creation, training and education in the community, Take Off Into Work has developed into a flagship scheme for the airport.

"The 600 successful candidates have been able to explore diverse career paths within this exciting industry, and I continue to follow their progression. Many more local job opportunities will be created, the City Airport Development Programme creating 500 jobs during the construction phase, with 1,600 jobs and as the airport grows."

Entrants in the Take Off Into Work scheme have secured jobs in departments across the airport including customer services, security and airfield operations as well as with other onsite employers such as airline cabin crew, passenger handling and the foreign exchange bureau.

Over three decades the airport has worked tirelessly in involving itself with numerous joint projects. In 2010 it gained the prestigious Lord Mayor of London's Dragon Award. This recognises the airport's significant contribution and commitment to the economic regeneration of London through the Take Off Into Work Programme which is aimed at young aspiring students.

In 2015 Parliament's All-Party Parliamentary Corporate Responsibility Group inaugurated the National Business Champion award.

The Speaker of the House of Commons John Bercow said: 'I congratulate London

Fun day was very busy on the apron.

City Airport on winning the 2015 National Responsible Business Champion award. It was described by Stephen Timms (MP for East Ham), a former Corporate Responsibility Minister, as an 'exemplar of corporate responsibility'.

The speaker cited LCY's investment in the local community; its commitment to providing pathways into work for unemployed residents; its work with schools and universities.

The momentum continues to be built, in 2016 some 4,241 students participating in LCY's educational programmes including 110 young people taking part in a new flagship science, technology, engineering and maths programme (STEM).

Work experience is another vital part of the CSR efforts and offering local college and university students a chance to participate in a week-long experience working alongside industry professionals in such areas as ramp operations, finance, customer services and the Private Jet Centre.

In 2017 more volunteers than ever before took part in London City Airport's annual Volunteering Fortnight, with 61 staff taking time out of their working weeks to participate in the initiative and make a meaningful contribution to local organisations and charities.

Airport employees from across all parts of the business volunteered at ten different community partners and charities in East London, dedicating their time, skills and expertise to activities and causes in six boroughs – Barking & Dagenham, Greenwich, Havering, Newham, Tower Hamlets and Waltham Forest.

It is the fourth year in a row that that the airport has organised the fortnight, coinciding with National Volunteers' Week, with eight of the activities set up in collaboration with the East London Business Alliance, including those at Barking Food Bank, Spitalfields City Farm, and the Waltham Forest Disability Resource Centre. Volunteering Fortnight is part of the airport's continued work and investment in local communities, with 2,333 hours volunteered in 2016, and came in the same month that the airport collected an award at the International CSR Excellence Awards 2017.

Local charities and organisations are eligible for the airport's 30th anniversary fund, a £30,000 endowment to support groups which enable significant and positive change for communities near London City Airport.

One of London City's proudest achievements has been its longstanding support for Richard House Children's Hospice, raising close to £900,000 since it first began fundraising initiatives over two decades ago. Sited just north of the Royal Albert Dock, by the Connaught Bridge, the residential unit provides care for children and young people who have life-limiting illnesses, and supporting their families. The children love to watch the aircraft landing and taking off.

On Friday 7 July 2017, 52 cyclists set off from London City in the July heat for a gruelling 185-mile bike ride to Amsterdam to raise money for the hospice. The airport is on course to raise £30,000 this year for the charity described by Stephen Timms, who took part, "as doing a tremendous job".

(Left to right) Sir Robin Wales (Mayor of Newham), the 600th recruit, Jasjoot Mudhar, a baggage tracing agent, and Declan Collier.

Chapter Seventeen
The Future of the Royals

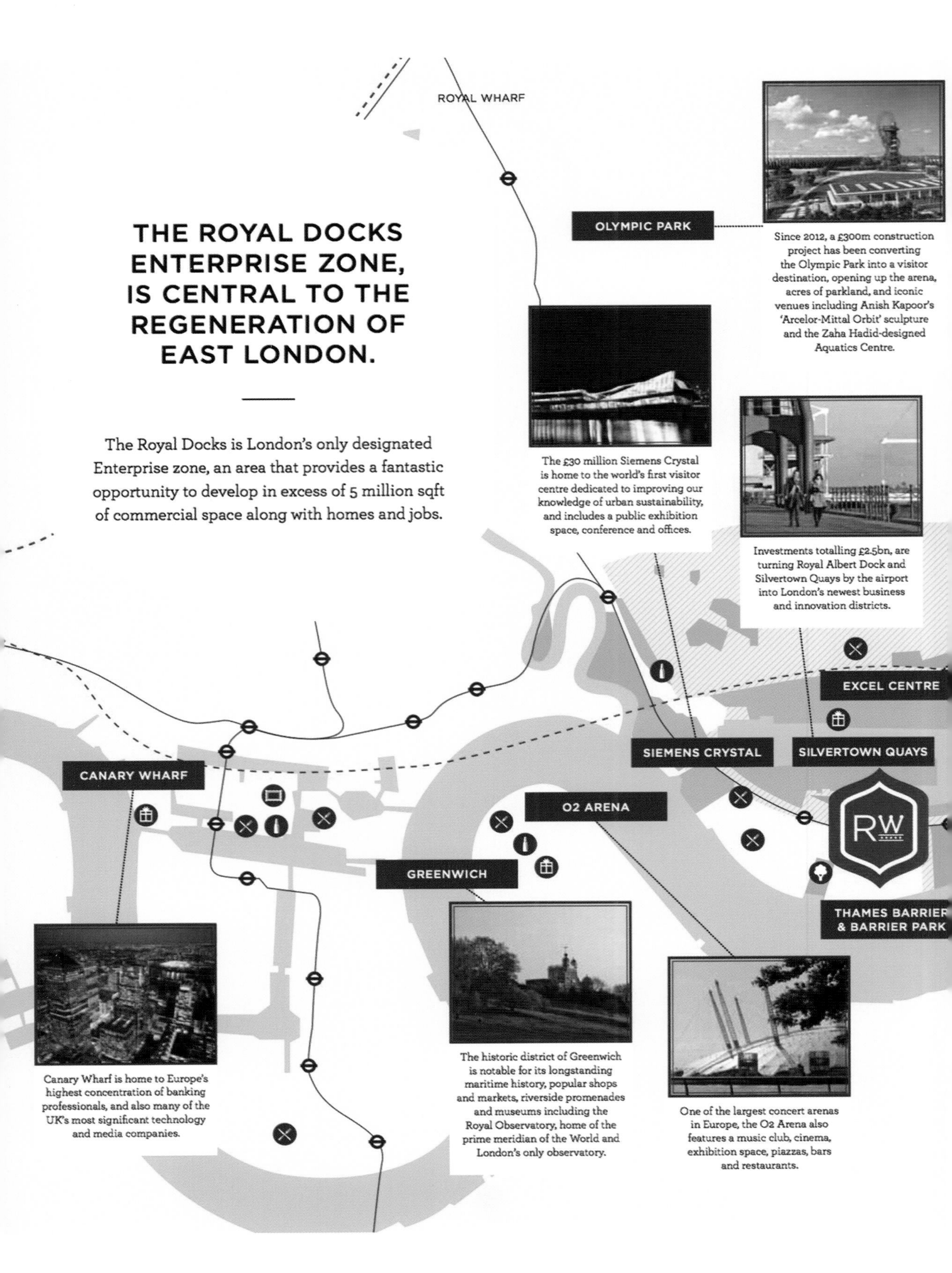

ROYAL WHARF
THE ROYAL DOCKS ENTERPRISE ZONE, IS CENTRAL TO THE REGENERATION OF EAST LONDON.
The Royal Docks is London's only designated Enterprise zone, an area that provides a fantastic opportunity to develop in excess of 5 million sqft of commercial space along with homes and jobs.
OLYMPIC PARK
Since 2012, a £300m construction project has been converting the Olympic Park into a visitor destination, opening up the arena, acres of parkland, and iconic venues including Anish Kapoor's 'Arcelor-Mittal Orbit' sculpture and the Zaha Hadid-designed Aquatics Centre.
The £30 million Siemens Crystal is home to the world's first visitor centre dedicated to improving our knowledge of urban sustainability, and includes a public exhibition space, conference and offices.
Investments totalling £2.5bn, are turning Royal Albert Dock and Silvertown Quays by the airport into London's newest business and innovation districts.
EXCEL CENTRE
SIEMENS CRYSTAL
SILVERTOWN QUAYS
CANARY WHARF
O2 ARENA
RW
GREENWICH
THAMES BARRIER & BARRIER PARK
Canary Wharf is home to Europe's highest concentration of banking professionals, and also many of the UK's most significant technology and media companies.
The historic district of Greenwich is notable for its longstanding maritime history, popular shops and markets, riverside promenades and museums including the Royal Observatory, home of the prime meridian of the World and London's only observatory.
One of the largest concert arenas in Europe, the O2 Arena also features a music club, cinema, exhibition space, piazzas, bars and restaurants.

ROYAL WHARF

ExCeL London plays a vital role in bringing business tourism to the Capital, generating over £1.6 billion in economic benefit.

In May 2013 the Mayor announced a £1bn investment by Chinese developer Advanced Business Parks (ABP) to turn the Royal Albert Dock site into London's next business district.

UEL is one of the top six modern universities for research in the country, with a Docklands campus that's home to a state-of-the-art sporting facility and business centre.

ASIAN BUSINESS PORT

UNIVERSITY OF EAST LONDON

LONDON CITY AIRPORT

From Amsterdam to New York, London City Airport offers quick and convenient flights to a large range of worldwide destinations.

The design icon that is the Thames Barrier opened in 1984, and when the Thames Barrier Park followed in 2000 it was the first new riverside park in London for over fifty years.

The Docklands Sailing and Watersports Centre offers sailing, windsurfing and powerboating among its series of Royal Yachting Association-recognised courses.

PUBLIC GREEN SPACES

EXISTING COMMUNITIES

CROSS RAIL (PLANNED)
The arrival of the Crossrail in 2018 will provide high speed links to central London and Heathrow.

Restaurant/ Cafe

Park

Sports

Museum/ Gallery

Bar/ Pub

Shopping

Mike Luddy, Managing Director, Royal Docks Management Authority Ltd (RoDMA), sits in his offices just by the River Thames lock entrance to the King George V Dock (the southern expanse of water at London City Airport).

He can watch aircraft on 'finals' for their approach to the airport and in the past has seen the big cruise ships manoeuvring as they made their way to the Royal Albert Dock (to the north of the London City runway) to berth as accommodation for the 2012 London Olympic Games. During The London Boat Show in January a whole fleet of boats and superyachts will pass by, and every other year for Defence and Security Equipment International (DSEI), an international navy flotilla. They will be making their way to the third of the Royal Docks, the Royal Victoria Dock, which now features ExCeL London.

Luddy is no stranger to aircraft, or vast engineering projects. Managing Director since June 2011, Mike's job is to lead the regeneration of what was one of Victorian England's greatest enterprises and at the time the greatest docks in the world.

An obvious choice, he knew London's eastern gateway well, previously leading a project to develop the Spectator Experience for the London Olympic Games. He had spent four years as Chief Commercial Officer at Gatwick Airport, responsible for some £400 million of revenue, and taking the airport through the £1.2 billion sale from BAA Plc to Global Infrastructure Partners (GIP). Previously, as Project Director for London and Continental Railways, Mike was responsible for devising and implementing the award-winning commercial and operational regeneration strategy for the iconic St Pancras International station which reopened on 14 November 2007.

In many ways RoDMA is a true successor to the London Docklands Development Corporation (LDDC) although not entrusted with any statutory authority. It maintains the lifting and swing bridges, the lock gates, pumping houses and other dock infrastructure. The three docks collectively once formed the largest enclosed docks in the world, with a water area of nearly 250 acres and an overall estate of 1,100 acres. This is equivalent to the whole of central London from Hyde Park to Tower Bridge. The area was designated a Special Enterprise Zone in 2012.

King George V Dock

Begun in 1912 by the Port of London Authority, the King George V was the last of London's upstream enclosed docks to be built. After delay by World War I, construction was completed in 1921. Although at 64 acres of water it was smaller than the other Royals, it had its own entrance from the Thames through a lock and bascule bridge. The dock could berth liners as large as the RMS *Mauretania*. At its western end was a large graving dock (since filled in) and machine shop used for ship repairs by Harland and Wolff. It closed to commercial traffic along with the other Royal Docks in the 1980s.

The dock's major feature today is London City Airport (LCY), whose single runway has been built on the length of the north side of the dock. The western end has been filled in and the airport terminal built on the filled area. The rest of the dock is still in water, acting as a buffer between the airport runway and the surrounding area. The southern quayside has been cleared of dock buildings and is now largely used as car parking for the airport with a hotel and other developments planned for the future. The London City Airport land extends as far as Sir Steve Redgrave Bridge at the eastern end of the dock.

***Above:** University of East London student housing northside, east end Royal Albert Dock.*

***Left:** Watching the aircraft fly over. The western end of the Royal Victoria Dock offers a man-made beach.*

Royal Victoria Dock

At the western extremity, Royal Victoria Dock brings thousands of visitors to exhibitions, events, water sports activities, bars, restaurants and gardens. ExCeL London comes under its remit and moored at the western end is the Good Hotel, actively promoted by RoDMA, part social enterprise and part a way of overcoming hotel accommodation needs. (See Chapter Eight on ExCeL London.)

At the eastern end the land surrounding the King George V lock makes it ideal for sizable marine projects (the Olympic Rings were built here). Facilities include access for cranes, metered electrical power and water, pump out facilities, quayside working areas, parking, equipment storage, 24-hour security, toilets for staff, refuelling and a staffed workboat.

RoDMA supervises three major enterprises with a total expanse of 14 million square feet.

The key to the whole rejuvenation of the eastern end of the docks was the development of the Docklands Light Railway (DLR) from Canning Town on both sides of the Royals opening at the end of 2005, to Beckton via Custom House (for ExCeL) in 1994 and to the far end of the King George V Dock via London City Airport effectively replacing the old North Woolwich station.

The Elizabeth Line (Crossrail) dissects the whole area with a station at Custom House (for ExCeL), dropping under the Connaught Bridge and resurfacing just past the London City Airport Private Jet Centre. There are no further stations until the railway reaches the other side of the river.

The University of East London campus, sited opposite the airport across the dock and well to the right opened in 1999, has 1,200 student rooms, together with shops, cafés and restaurant, launderette and an open-air fitness suite. The SportsDock, a £21 million sports and academic centre, opened in March 2012. It served as the High-Performance Training Centre for Team USA during the London 2012 Olympic Games.

Cyprus station of the DLR, on the Beckton extension is adjacent to the campus, making access very easy.

Royal Albert Dock

Launched in October 2016 with great aplomb at the Mansion House by President Xi Jinping of China, alongside UK Prime Minister David Cameron, the £1.7 billion Advanced Business

Park (ABP) sits to the north of the Royal Albert Dock facing London City Airport. Its stated aim was as a launch for Chinese and Asian businesses into Europe. The Brexit vote and change of Prime Minister in June 2017 caused what turned out to be a blip and work is progressing at speed. The deal will make the project the biggest real estate development delivered in the UK by a Chinese construction company. It will be worth £6 billion to the United Kingdom economy creating 30,000 new jobs.

ABP joined forces with CITIC Group, the largest conglomerate in China and an established global player, with businesses covering financial services, resources and energy, manufacturing, engineering contracting and real estate. It is ranked in the top 200 of the Fortune Global 500 List.

Work is now well under way with the plan to deliver more than 600,000 square feet office space before the end of 2018. It will take 6–8 years to complete the scheme.

Silvertown (Pontoon Dock)

Directly to the east of the airport is Silvertown area, being delivered by The Silvertown Partnership, a consortium consisting of Chelsfield Properties, First Base and Macquarie Capital, all in themselves substantial and experienced property developers. The site is the biggest in the Docks at 62 acres of brownfield land with only three existing buildings.

In April 2015, Newham Council gave outline planning permission for a new £3.5 billion redevelopment of the area, including Millennium Mills. The iconic 500,000 square feet building is destined to become a centre for start-up businesses. Work began in January 2015 to clear the building of asbestos, following an initial £12 million grant from the Government.

The first phase of the development will deliver 5,000 new jobs, 1 million square feet of commercial space and 850 new homes. This will start to be available from 2019 onwards.

Every year, The Silvertown Partnership along with the Greater London Authority; who are the landowners open Millennium Mills and Silvertown to the public as part of the annual Open House London weekend. Visitors get to see firsthand the scale of the building, hear about its significance to the area and the plans to transform it into a hub alongside restaurants, bars and even a roof-top social space.

When complete, Silvertown will deliver 5 million square feet of commercial space and over 3,000 homes. This new community will employ over 21,000 people and contribute over £260 million in additional revenue for London.

In 2014, Singapore-listed Oxley Holdings, together with leading Irish developer Ballymore, announced a joint venture to develop a new waterfront township of Royal Wharf, situated on the River Thames between West Silvertown and Pontoon Dock stations on the DLR, with 3,385 new homes housing over 10,000 residents. Royal Wharf is a mixed-use development comprising homes, shops, restaurants and offices. The final phase is known as Mariner's Quarter which has the tallest building standing at 19 storeys, overlooking the River Thames and Canary Wharf. The development is situated between Barrier Park and Lyle Park, with 45% of the site given over to public space including a 2.4-acre park, pocket parks and garden squares.

To put the Royal Docks in true perspective the huge complex is expected to generate more some £15bn of industrial developments, 40,000 jobs, 4.000 homes over next 10–12 years. In East London 262,220 new homes and 210,950 new jobs are expected by 2035. London City Airport sits in the middle of it all.

Left: *Royal Victoria with the Emirates Air Bridge in the far background.*

THE TOP 20 ROUTES TO AND FROM LONDON CITY AIRPORT 2016

	Airport	Total passengers	% Change 2015–2016
1	Edinburgh	528,029	▼ 0.9
2	Amsterdam	517,305	▲ 6.0
3	Dublin	449,657	▼ 0.4
4	Zürich	385,933	▼ 2.9
5	Frankfurt	241,084	▲ 0.0
6	Glasgow	235,075	▼ 1.4
7	Rotterdam	219,857	▲ 5.3
8	Geneva	219,607	▲ 24.5
9	Luxembourg	183,097	▼ 2.1
10	Milan Linate	180,068	▲ 9.7
11	Belfast City	111,944	▼ 2.6
12	Paris Orly	111,015	▼ 9.9
13	Florence	98,773	▲ 3.2
14	Ibiza	88,376	▲ 16.9
15	Düsseldorf	74,580	▲ 24.7
16	Isle of Man	74,001	▲ 26.0
17	Madrid	70,900	▼ 15.4
18	Aberdeen	64,452	▲ 1.6
19	Málaga	57,772	▲ 11.4
20	Antwerp	54,885	▼ 6.3

30 YEARS OF SERVING LONDON
• Voted Best Regional Airport in the world*
• Only 20 mins from terminal entrance to departure lounge
• On arrival, just 15 minutes from plane to train
22 mins to Bank
25 mins to Westminster
14 mins to Canary Wharf
30 Years 1987-2017
London City Airport
Get closer.
London City Airport
Get closer.
FAST, PUNCTUAL AND ACTUALLY IN LONDON.
For timetables and bookings visit:
londoncityairport.com
*CAPA Regional Airport of the Year Award - 27/10/2016